Whiteness in America

Whiteness in America

Monica McDermott

polity

First published in 2020 by Polity Press

Polity Press
65 Bridge Street
Cambridge CB2 1UR, UK

Polity Press
101 Station Landing
Suite 300
Medford, MA 02155, USA

ISBN-13: 978-0-7456-7218-2
ISBN-13: 978-0-7456-7219-9(pb)

A catalogue record for this book is available from the British Library.

Library of Congress Cataloging-in-Publication Data
Names: McDermott, Monica, 1971- author.
Title: Whiteness in America / Monica McDermott.
Description: Cambridge, UK ; Medford, MA : Polity, 2020. | Includes
    bibliographical references and index. | Summary: "The invisible root of
    racial inequality"-- Provided by publisher.
Identifiers: LCCN 2020000124 (print) | LCCN 2020000125 (ebook) | ISBN
    9780745672182 (hardback) | ISBN 9780745672199 (pb) | ISBN 9781509531189 (epub)
Subjects: LCSH: Whites--Race identity--United States. | United States--Race
    relations--Social aspects. | Race awareness--United States. |
    Equality--United States.
Classification: LCC E184.A1 M3475 2020 (print) | LCC E184.A1 (ebook) |
    DDC 305.802973--dc23
LC record available at https://lccn.loc.gov/2020000124
LC ebook record available at https://lccn.loc.gov/2020000125

Typeset in 11 on 13pt Sabon
by Fakenham Prepress Solutions, Fakenham, Norfolk NR21 8NL
Printed and bound in Great Britain by TJ International Limited

For further information on Polity, visit our website:
politybooks.com

Contents

Acknowledgments

This book reflects the many conversations I have had with colleagues and students over the years. In particular, the students in my seminar on whiteness at the University of Illinois communicated the importance of understanding the manifestations of white privilege in their lives. Additionally, Helen Marrow provided useful comments, as did Jonathan Skerrett and two anonymous reviewers. Finally, I thank Rebecca Sandefur for her detailed comments, support, and encouragement.

– 1 –
Introduction

When Americans think about race, "white" is often the furthest thing from their minds. To have a race is to be black, Asian, Latina/o or American Indian. Yet whiteness colors so much of social life in the United States, from the organization and maintenance of social structures to an individual's sense of self. Why is there such a disconnect?

Before being able to answer this question, it is important to understand just what the term "white" means. Determining who is considered white—or black, or American Indian, or any other race—may seem obvious. In common conversation, people are said to appear visually as though they belong to a particular race. So, for example, membership in the category "white" is automatic if one has light skin, straight hair, and blue eyes. However, it is not the case that the possession of a given set of physical attributes automatically designates membership of a particular racial group. The meaning of race and any corresponding physical identifiers are deeply embedded in power relations (Omi 2001). This construction of whiteness is a central part of the social construction of race itself. Race is a result of social relations, not simply a reflection of the enduring attributes of any particular group of people. Hence the category "white" changes its meaning and shifts its boundaries in different times and places. Sometimes it goes unnoticed by the majority group, while at other times whites are readily seen, even by themselves.

Although the privilege of whiteness has touched, in some way, every part of the globe, its manifestation in America is relatively unique. European colonialism led to an equation between "race" and dominance, as settler colonists from Europe oppressed and exploited non-European (and therefore non-white) residents throughout the world. One of the starkest examples of this exploitation was the slave trade. The extensive transport of slaves to the United States—coupled with a relatively large population of European origin—led to the development of a society that was built upon racial violence and subordination. The genocide of indigenous populations further solidified the power of whites, who, given their numeric majority, were less threatened by a non-white revolution than were their counterparts in other countries. In America, not only is whiteness synonymous with privilege, but the mobilization and defense of whites' interests have fundamentally shaped every aspect of life. Even the initial ethnic differences among European settlers slowly blurred, creating one uniform "white" group—at which point whiteness became increasingly associated with intelligence and a strong work ethic (Levine-Rasky 2016). As the privileges of whiteness grew greater, the desire of individuals to be included within this group became stronger.

The boundaries of whiteness have been vigorously policed by a variety of American institutions. López (2006; originally published in 1996) provides a compelling account of the ways in which racial categories have been constructed by social institutions, especially the law, in the face of individual pressure for inclusion. In addition to legal measures, "white" has also been a subject of contestation in educational institutions, neighborhoods, social organizations, government policy, the media, and innumerable personal interactions in daily life. As Jacobson (1999) has demonstrated, the racialization of Jews is a particularly illustrative example of the ways in which whiteness is articulated and policed and, ultimately, of how malleable it is. While anti-Semitic movements and ideologies are still evident in contemporary America, Jews' identification as white is assumed by all but the most extreme white supremacists. Yet there was a time less than a century ago when Jews were often considered to be non-white. One example of the discriminatory treatment that Jews received during that time comes from elite colleges and universities that had quotas designed to restrict the number of Jewish matriculates (Karabel 2005). Jewish fraternities arose in response to the exclusion of Jews from white social organizations (Sanua 2018). And restrictive covenants prevented Jews from buying homes in a number of neighborhoods throughout the country (Brooks and Rose 2013).

To many, these structural impediments to the economic and social opportunities of Jews might seem surprising. The fact that they are surprising is testament to the shifting boundaries of whiteness. But, while these boundaries may have shifted, one fact remains constant: whiteness is a definitive mark of privilege. Individuals and groups have fought bitterly for inclusion in the category of "white" for precisely this reason.

The whiteness that so many have striven to obtain has multiple manifestations. Perhaps the most important is the aforementioned privilege attached to this category. Ultimately, whiteness manifests itself in all circumstances as privilege, even if individuals may not view it as such. As critical race theorists note, "racial stratification is ordinary, ubiquitous, and reproduced in mundane and extraordinary customs and experience" (Brown 2008: 54). The privilege of whiteness is so interwoven with the "normal" functioning of institutions and the character of interactions that it is often noticed only in cases of rupture of the ordinary, for example when white supremacists use a racial slur. However, the power and privilege of whiteness do not require that overt racism survive; rather, advantages accrue to whites because the economic, political and social institutions of America have long been designed to secure white dominance. This may take the form of discrimination in lending, voter disenfranchisement, and a host of other ways that are not the product of individuals' overt racism.

White identity is connected to privilege, as it is shaped in the set of social relations and interactions that are connected to white dominance. However, identity is typically formed at the individual level, so there is variation in the ways in which whites understand the meaning of their racial group membership. Some whites rarely think about their racial identity and may in fact believe that they have no race; this belief is, itself, a form of identity. Some whites may feel strongly attached to being white, either from a sense of pride (which can be connected to white supremacist affiliations) or from a sense of guilt (which can spur some whites down the path of anti-racist activism). White identity is important to understand, as it is connected to a host of political and social behaviors.

For example, attitudes toward non-white racial groups, immigration, and criminal justice policies can be influenced by white identity. In general, whites are more likely to be punitive toward those caught in the criminal justice system on the offending side, and they are also more likely to be opposed to immigration. Some of the attitudes whites hold toward non-whites—especially blacks and Latinos/as—are related to feelings of threat in front of a perceived loss of status and control (Craig and Richeson 2014b). In general, familiarity with white attitudes can provide the basis for understanding white behavior; changing attitudes can change actions, which in turn can reduce the ways in which whites act to maintain their privilege. In some cases, whites' attitudes can lead them to affiliate with social movements that are designed to extend, secure, or challenge the benefits of whiteness. Some of the organizations that will be discussed later, such as the Tea Party, the Ku Klux Klan, and the liberal Center for a Fair Economy, are motivated by different dimensions of whiteness to shape their policies and actions.

Discussions of race and privilege can founder on notions that privilege is roughly equivalent to being rich—that privilege is an outcome rather than a structural position. This understanding of privilege suggests that there is no connection between race and privilege—that any group is equally able to make money through hard work and good choices. In addition, those adopting an individual-level understanding of race and privilege might point to the many whites who are *not* economically advantaged but have to struggle through their daily lives. How could such struggles possibly indicate privilege? However, privilege is much broader than simply a reflection of one's income (Kimmel and Ferber 2009). Whites are advantaged over non-whites in myriad ways that apply to *all* whites, not just to those with a lot of money and education. It is important to note that whites are privileged relatively to non-whites not merely through the direct benefits of whiteness, but also through its function as a category of structural power and control. Regardless of the personal difficulties that an individual white person might experience, he or she is, ultimately, the beneficiary of his or her group's dominant status. Access to resources and opportunities is substantially greater for members of the dominant group *even if specific individuals are unable to take advantage of it.* Just as all citizens of the United States benefit from the superior military defense of the nation when it comes to being protected from invasion, all whites benefit from the superior structural position of their group when it comes to the types of systematic advantage that this position grants them.

The benefits of structural advantage are often understood in monetary terms: whites make more money and have more wealth than blacks or Latinos/as. Thinking about racial advantage in terms of money is illuminating, but it can encourage people to explain away class differences as attached to individual-level characteristics—a strong work ethic or high intelligence, for instance. Evidence suggests that the source of racial advantage need not rest with the individual at all. For example, Royster's (2003) study of racial differences in the social networks that help workers secure employment shows that whites have advantages over blacks without even trying. Whites refer friends for jobs, and the racial segregation of many friendship groups means that white people's friends are typically white. Even in a group of similarly trained, similarly skilled black and white working-class men who graduated from the same high school in Baltimore, whites had higher status jobs and shorter periods of unemployment. This racial difference in work opportunities was due almost exclusively to the different informal networks to which black and white men had access (Royster 2003).

Social networks are not the only structural factor creating the advantages of whiteness. Home ownership is the primary source of wealth for most Americans (Krivo and Kaufman 2004), and homes in majority black neighborhoods are likely to be devalued by comparison to homes in white-dominated neighborhoods—even after holding other housing and community characteristics constant (Perry, Rothwell, and Harshbarger 2018). In addition, blacks are less likely to have access to loans or gifts from family members that could help them make a down payment on a home. At every step of the home-buying process—from finding a real estate agent through having a mortgage application evaluated to closing the sale—they are victims of stereotypes and discrimination that give whites unfair access to resources and space (Korver-Glenn 2018). Delays in stepping into home ownership, coupled with slowly increasing (or even decreasing) property values, can make an initially small (or relatively small) racial gap in wealth between a white and a black individual become a huge difference by the end of life. This disadvantage is transmitted to the next generation and can accumulate throughout time even without any active discrimination.

Other forms of the structural advantage of whiteness are manifested in more subtle ways. The social burden of dealing with discrimination and reduced opportunities takes a toll on the health and well-being of many non-white groups. African Americans in particular have lower life expectancies than whites, even after controlling for social class (Franks et al. 2006). In and of itself, the process of dealing with the stress of increased scrutiny and lowered expectations can result in an increased likelihood of a host of medical conditions such as heart disease and depression. The fact that more blacks are concentrated in low-income groups that tend to live shorter lives than the affluent explains some health discrepancies, but there is also an independent contribution of race to health outcomes. For example, blacks who live in relatively affluent neighborhoods and suffer a heart attack live for fewer years afterwards than do whites who live in relatively affluent neighborhoods (Bucholz et al. 2015).

While these structural advantages of whiteness are fundamental, racial identity is also important to individuals' conceptualization and understanding of themselves; it is a substantial component of whiteness. "Whiteness" and "white identity" can be used somewhat interchangeably, although identity refers more precisely to a conceptualization of race that centers on an individual, while whiteness encompasses the broader racialization of structures, culture, and institutions that manifest white racial privilege and expression. Identity, in other words, is how we (and others) think about our own relationship to racial categories, while whiteness is a broader concept, which includes both individual and societal racial definitions and processes.

Psychological as well as social benefits can be attached to racial identification. White identities—even when not consciously assimilated—can make individuals feel that they are normal and unremarkable. White identity facilitates other, non-racial identities to take on greater importance in white people's lives. For example gender, sexual orientation, religion, political party, and region of residence are given the space to be prominent features of individuals' lives. For many blacks, Latinos/as, American Indians, and Asians, on the other hand, racial identity is linked so prominently to daily experiences that it can be a near-totalizing component of their broader identity. Non-white identities need not be negative, however. People who do not identify as white can have a sense of pride and enhanced self-esteem as a result of their racial identities (Hughes et al. 2015).

While racial identity manifests itself differently not only among different subgroups of whites, it can do so for the same individual, over time. Knowing how whites understand what their racial identification means to them is important for a host of reasons. Self-identification with any group influences the ways in which we view the world and our place in it. It also influences the ways in which we treat members of other groups. Even when identity remains unacknowledged, it is nonetheless implicit, as individuals explicitly exclude themselves from other identities. For example, even though a middle-class white individual living in a racially homogenous neighborhood might explicitly identify as white only on rare occasions, such as when filling out a survey form (Martin et al. 1999) or a job application, their white identity is always implicit in their conceptualization of themselves as "not black" or "not Latino/a."

It is important to think about the different ways in which white racial identity manifests itself across the broad, eclectic spectrum of those considered (by themselves and by others) "white." By categorizing different understandings and experiences of whiteness, we can not only gain a deeper appreciation of racial self-awareness but also make linkages between forms of identity and social and political behavior. It is easy to be baffled by sudden acts of racial violence or by white assertions of superiority, especially as they coexist with white anti-racist activism and a desire to "save" poor blacks and Latinos/as from their difficult circumstances. What leads people to mobilize their racial identities in such different ways? Why aren't all white people alike?

There are a range of answers to these questions. Social class, geography, social context, and degree of contact with non-whites all influence white racial identity. It is especially important to think about the ways in which the contexts and the statuses of others affect whiteness, as these ways demonstrate that whiteness is not a "natural, unchangeable phenomenon" (Alcoff 2015: 74). Contexts such as neighborhood choice not only are influenced by white identity but also shape it (Alcoff 2015). For example, whites who live in majority non-white neighborhoods or work in majority non-white settings will be routinely reminded of their whiteness, as it makes them stand in opposition to those with whom they frequently interact. In such settings, interactions between whites and non-whites can have a multilayered quality, shaped by class and spatial factors as they intersect with abstract understandings of race (Hartigan 1997). The same would be true of whites married to non-whites. White racial awareness will most likely be much greater among them than among the many whites who work, attend school and live in primarily white settings. Vasquez (2014) refers to this awareness as "racial cognizance," a perspective that not only entails an awareness of white identity but also is explicitly aware of racial inequality. In the case of whites married to Latinos/as, the awareness of whiteness is generated not only by the continual contrasting racial classifications of those in one's immediate environment, but also by the incidence of witnessing instances of discrimination against family members (Vasquez 2014).

Whiteness manifests itself differently in different regions of the country, racial identity often being experienced differently in the South and in the Southwest, for example. In addition, rural whites can have a different understanding of what it means to be white—different, that is, from that of urban or suburban dwellers. In part, this is a result of exposure to non-whites; many rural areas, especially those outside the South, tend to be racially isolated. Even though suburbs can be just as isolated, many residents commute to cities that have larger, often visible non-white populations. Regionally, the non-white groups that predominate can be quite different; thus whites might be counterpoised to American Indians in the Plains states, to Latinos/as in the Southwest and in the West, to Asians in the West, and to blacks in the South, Northeast, and Midwest. Owing to the association that many whites make between Latinos/as and Asians and immigration status and that prompts them to "over-include" devalued groups within the immigrant category (Kosic and Phalet 2006), whites in the West and Southwest who interact with large Asian and Latino/a populations there might attach a nativist or nationalist meaning to whiteness. Whites in the South have a very long history of living with a rigid racial dichotomy between whites and blacks that has structured every aspect of daily life. It is reasonable to expect vestiges of this rigid dichotomy to set strong boundaries around whiteness today.

Important contextual effects that vary across cities—such as demographics, segregation, or inequality—can also vary across neighborhoods *within* a single city. Doering's (2015) study of "positive loiterers"—whites who congregate in public in order to deter people from criminal activity— shows that whites located in multiracial contexts have a visibility to their whiteness that others—whites in homogenous neighborhoods, or in less public settings—do not. The ways in which these whites navigate their identities varies. One group anticipated racial challenges and engaged with critics, while another isolated itself from blacks in the neighborhood and dismissed those who confronted it. These cases point to the importance of context in shaping expressions of whiteness (Doering 2015).

Although context is certainly important in shaping white identities, the reach of whiteness transcends the particular and is both the cause and the consequence of the larger structural forces that shape identities. While it might seem unusual to assert that an identity can change a structural force, political and economic conditions can be reinforced, or even transformed, by the patterned behaviors of whites as they enact their identities. For example, white superiority can facilitate the passage of legislation that results in the criminalization or disenfranchisement of non-whites. This legislation, in turn, can solidify, or even generate, whites' feelings of moral superiority over other racial groups. So, too, can broader patterns of residential segregation influence whiteness. For example, racial segregation can mitigate against positive attitudes to immigration among whites (Rocha and Espino 2009). Similarly, racially homogenous neighborhoods can undergird a sense of having rights to certain areas, which are then thought to exist primarily for whites. These perceived rights can prompt white residents to call the police on a black pedestrian in "their" neighborhood. The white identities that emerge from these patterns of segregation and their corresponding behaviors, in turn, reify racialized neighborhood boundaries and have a cascading effect on the segregation of other institutions such as schools.

Colorblind identities such as those generated by racially homogenous neighborhoods are reflected in whites' inability to see their own race as an important factor in their lives. Race is instead thought to be a characteristic that non-whites have; whites simply do not think of themselves as having a race at all. One of the reasons why whiteness often goes unremarked is the widely held assumption that "white" is the norm—the default racial category in America. This reality is generated by a long history of white racial dominance, in which whites have controlled institutions, shaped the culture, and enforced their power through a variety of mechanisms. As a result, they have been in a position to defend their rights and power by drawing boundaries around their group, such that white became the norm and all other groups fell outside of the norm. The invisibility of whiteness is such that the privilege it involves is often hidden from view—it seems like the natural order of things. This invisibility of whiteness is especially common among whites in racially homogenous settings: when white is the norm and no stimulus is activating racial identity, one's own race is seen as a non-factor. Given the high degree of residential and educational segregation in the United States, this experience of whiteness is, indeed, the "norm."

As discussed earlier, privilege refers to the often unseen benefits of occupying a structurally rewarded position in society such as being white, or male, or heterosexual. The benefits of privilege are many, ranging from a greater likelihood of earning extra income to a greater likelihood of getting away with shoplifting than those without privilege. The very category of "white" is based on the existence of privilege in relation to people of color. The boundaries of whiteness have reflected a history of groups striving for inclusion in the category of "white" and the corresponding high status and resources that being white bestows (Roediger 1991). To be white is to have the opportunity to be included in the civic, political and economic life of the nation. White is the default category against which other racial and ethnic groups are measured. Yet few of those within this category see their racial experience as anything but the norm; it is the others whom they regard as different.

Among the first to observe this power of whiteness in America was the sociologist W. E. B. DuBois. In *The Souls of White Folk*, DuBois noted that the overt racial dominance claimed by the white race ultimately came to manifest itself in subtler ways, as the notion that all that is right, good, and powerful equals white came to be taken for granted.

How easy ... by emphasis and omission to make children believe that every great soul the world ever saw was a white man's soul; that every great thought the world ever knew was a white man's thought; that every great deed the world ever did was a white man's deed; that every great dream the world ever sang was a white man's dream. (DuBois 1996: 498)

The books and lessons children of all races receive have been filled with white faces, the images representing America are white faces (such as that of Uncle Sam), and "white" is rarely used as a racial descriptor. One hears of a "black scientist" or a "Mexican actor" but not of a white scientist or white actor—the whiteness of scientists and actors is often simply assumed.

However, some whites have a strong sense of their own racial identity. Rather than assuming that they are simply people without any race, they are instead acutely aware of the role that whiteness plays in their lives. White identity can actually have a *negative* impact on individuals' sense of self. For example, poor and working-class whites can be negatively affected by their racial identity when they are judged harshly by others for not capitalizing on the socioeconomic benefits of whiteness (Hartigan 1999; McDermott 2006). Indeed, social class can have a major impact on how whites understand their racial identities. The stigma of poverty attaches to every low-income person regardless of race, but poor whites must deal with an additional judgment. Since whiteness is associated with affluence and privilege, poor whites are often seen as being especially damaged or defective. If they were "real" whites, who work hard and are intelligent, they would have moved up and out of poverty. Whites are effectively seen as having no excuse for being poor, since their skin color should have guaranteed better socio-economic outcomes (McDermott 2006). The combined stigma against poor whites is so prevalent that a special term—"white trash"—has emerged to dismiss and malign whites with little money or education.

Whites can feel stigmatized for their white identity from a quite different source—one not related to social class directly. As mentioned previously, "white guilt" can manifest itself when individuals confront the reality of their privilege and are aware of the undeserved advantages it has brought and continues to bring in their lives. Despite there being no mismatch between their socioeconomic status and their racial identity, these whites nonetheless attach a negative valence to the latter. Especially among non-whites and among white anti-racist activists, whiteness itself can be an inherently stigmatized identity. Some anti-racist activists actually engage in strategies in order to embrace this stigma (Hughey 2012a). The mixed-race women that Storrs (1999) interviewed took the opposite approach; although all the women had white ancestry, they were disgusted by whiteness as "oppressive, patriarchal and discriminatory" (Storrs 1999: 196).

At the same time, whiteness can be *embraced* as a marker of difference, a marker that many bitterly fight to keep distinctive. The construction of this difference extends back to the earliest period of European coloni- zation of the United States, when it was a marker of status and power. While whiteness is often invisible to those who consider themselves whites, it is not always the case that it goes unnoticed. For example blacks, Latinos/as, American Indians and Asians often notice whiteness; for many of them, successfully negotiating the social and institutional worlds of America requires recognizing whiteness so as to avoid negative outcomes. But whites, too, are sometimes cognizant of their racial identity. When confronted with a perceived threat to their racial advantages—such as blacks moving into a white majority neighborhood—whites may consciously mobilize on the basis of race, in order to organize resistance to neighborhood change.

Such neighborhood characteristics, which influence white racial identity, are fairly stable, but the meanings of whiteness can also be shaped by the specific settings in which whites interact with others. For example, the mentioning of racialized issues such as crime, schools, and neighborhoods can heighten awareness of whiteness even if no other non-whites are present. This awareness can take the form of superiority or defensiveness, as whites become conscious of threats to their status or reinforcements of their dominant position in society. For example, whites who are prompted to think about or discuss the racial composition of neighborhoods or schools might feel threatened by the changing demographics of the US, worrying that white spaces and institutions are changing to be less the province of whites (Craig and Richeson 2014a). Alternatively, contexts in which crime is discussed might arouse in whites a sense of superiority over blacks and Latinos/as: in these contexts whiteness can be stereotypically equated with law-abiding, pro-social behavior, in direct contrast to the presumed criminal behavior of blacks and Latinos/as. It need not matter, for this experience of white racial identity, what the actual association between race and crime is; it is rather the perceptions and the attitudes that have such a powerful impact.

Some whites become so conscious of their whiteness that they actually seek to transcend it, to identify with an entirely different race. Some whites feel guilty about the unearned privileges they have and consciously try to counteract these advantages by affiliating themselves with non-whites, or by participating in anti-racist efforts. Others, who had long thought of themselves as white (and whom others thought of as white), "discover," by taking a DNA test, that they are not white at all. The presence of American Indian or African origin DNA sometimes prompts such whites to leave their old race behind and adopt a new identity (Roth and Ivemark 2018), thus transcending their whiteness (although not their white privilege).

Regardless of whether white people's identities are colorblind, stigmatized, defensive, or transcendent, these people's ways of thinking about themselves shape their attitudes toward other racial groups. However, the connection between identities and attitudes is not straightforward. Among people who identify as white, it is not the case that those who are most likely to acknowledge that their white identity is important to them are the most (or the least) racist groups of whites. Instead, the ways in which whites think about the meaning of whiteness influences their orientations toward other groups. For example, an individual who does not consider his or her whiteness to be symbolic of anything and goes through life blissfully unaware of his or her own race is unlikely to understand the profound influence of race on the daily lives of many non-whites. On the other hand, an individual who fully embraces the social dominance associated with whiteness is much more likely to assert his or her identity as a mark of superiority, or even supremacy. Whites who acknowledge their social dominance and still find it problematic can engage in anti-racist activism or paternalistic behavior toward non-whites. In Chapter 4 there will be a review of the identity–attitude connection in survey responses, discussing how whites who have a strong sense of their identity are among both the most and the least likely to have positive attitudes toward blacks.

Attitudes expressed in survey data are only one way of measuring how whites understand the world around them. Whiteness is expressed culturally as well. If one thinks of culture as patterned behaviors and preferences, it can be a useful vehicle for understanding the relationship between structure and identity. While we often associate culture with forms such as music and film, it also applies to styles of relating to others, for instance to speech and dress, or to ways in which people enact their goals. The extent to which there is a "white" culture has been debated. Certain musical forms, such as country and, to a lesser extent, classical music, have been deemed to be a part of white culture on the basis of the themes and styles of their production as well as of the demographics of its audiences. More troubling, white supremacist groups have extolled the virtues and achievements of European culture as a reflection of the greatness of "white culture" (Dentice and Bugg 2016).

Different cultures can also be expressed within social movements that go well beyond a set of preferences and patterned behaviors. Such movements are goal-oriented, organized institutional forms, which can serve as bases for the realization of the interests of dominant groups such as whites. In some cases, such as that of the Ku Klux Klan, these goals are pursued through violence. In others, the attempted realization of the goals that serve white interests is non-violent and the articulation of whiteness's role within the movement is subtler. Such organized movements can lay bare the ways in which whiteness is a major actor in the political and social arenas in America today.

Movements organized around racial goals are likely to become increasingly prevalent as the demographic changes occurring in the US continue. The white population is becoming a smaller part of the overall American population, with Latinos/as in particular making up a larger proportion. By the mid-century, whites are predicted to represent a minority of the country's population. Much of this growth in the non-white population is fueled by immigration, although a not inconsiderable amount is also generated by a rapidly increasing multiracial population. Depending on the extent to which multiracial individuals and members of some immigrant groups racially identify as white in the future, the white population might not be declining that much, after all (Alba 2016). Just as the boundaries of whiteness expanded in the early twentieth century to include Jews, Italians and other European immigrants who were considered not quite white, so too might groups currently considered non-white be regarded as white in the near future. Alternatively, however, Fox and Guglielmo (2012) argue that European immigrants were never actually outside the white racial boundary; their experience, therefore, has little to tell us about the future white racialization of other groups.

In general, the story of whiteness is both one of structures of oppression that extend back to the founding of America and one of a rapidly changing set of complex identities, which lead simultaneously to conflict and cooperation in contemporary life. In order to understand the ways in which these rigid structures and complicated perceptions permeate American life, we must examine some of the many meanings of what it is to be white—including the racial privilege inherent to them all.

The rest of the book discusses the various manifestations and implications of whiteness in America. Chapter 2 presents the concept of "invisible privilege." As mentioned earlier, many whites are unaware of how they benefit from their whiteness. How does this happen? The chapter describes the origins of beliefs about race and racial identity among whites by reviewing some of the ways in which white children learn about race. While most children are not directly instructed about the meaning of whiteness, they absorb many messages from their parents and from their school environments. They carry these messages into adulthood, where they apply the lessons to their own understandings of American society as basically "colorblind," a place where race holds little relevance. Colorblindness often masquerades as a seemingly desirable belief about every individual being like every other individual, but this universalist belief actually hides a dismissal of the importance of racism in the lives of non-whites. If we are all the same and we all have equal chances to get ahead, then non-whites can be assumed to deserve having lower incomes and a lower educational attainment. "Not seeing color" can mean not seeing inequality. Finally, Chapter 2 reviews the concept of "hegemonic whiteness." The theory behind this concept points out the ways in which whiteness is interwoven throughout American society such that it is not noticed. Furthermore, the use of whiteness to negatively influence the lives of most Americans—including many whites—is often accepted as a part of "normal" society.

While invisible whiteness is an important and perhaps dominant form of whiteness, Chapter 3 discusses the ways in which whiteness can be *visible*. In certain places and situations, whites are quite aware of their racial identity. One example of visible whiteness is that of stigmatized whites. These are individuals who have one or more characteristics that reflect a relative lack of power or standing. For example, the case of poor whites discussed earlier involves people who are both privileged through their whiteness and disadvantaged through their class status. Since one stereotype of whites is that they are affluent and successful, the racial status of poor whites tends to get highlighted: such people tend to be seen as not living up to their racial standing. They may be thought to have done something to deserve their poverty, since discrimination would not be to blame. It is not only to stigmatized whites that race is salient, however. Sometimes whites assert their racial privilege in a way that makes their identity salient to themselves and others. Whites who organize in order to keep non-whites out of the neighborhoods they live in are consciously exercising their racial privilege rather than living their lives in an entirely color-blind fashion. Finally, some whites actually try to abandon their white identity, claiming to have an entirely different racial background. The widespread adoption of DNA testing has increased the number of whites who, in the light of new information, think of themselves as belonging to other racial groups. Other whites are sharply aware of their white privilege and attempt to change its meaning. In all the cases discussed in Chapter 3, white racial identity is salient, not hidden.

Chapter 4 presents some of the ways in which whiteness influences attitudes on a range of topics. It also discusses the influence of culture on experiences with and the diffusion of whiteness. Patterned beliefs and practices not only are a result of white identity; they also shape it. Several different theories of white racial attitudes engage with the ways in which whiteness symbolizes a sense of cultural superiority, as well as with the role played by the degree of possessiveness expressed by whites in the face of perceived political and economic threats. White attitudes are not limited to whites' thinking about race, however. Whites are also unique in their support for the harsh treatment of those arrested and incarcerated—attitudes that a number of scholars have demonstrated are racialized. The cultural practices of whites diverge in some cases from the practices of other groups. While this occurs in a variety of dimensions, one example that will be discussed is that of country music.

Chapter 5 discusses the ways in which white identity and privilege are mobilized. Often, when Americans think about the ways in which white people join social movements to further the interests of their race, they think about white supremacist movements. The Ku Klux Klan, neo-Nazis, and other supremacist groups are indeed important organizations to understand. However, there are other ways in which whiteness is connected to whites' involvement in social movements. Some organizations, such as the Tea Party movement, comprise a large majority of white members. More importantly, however, their goals would secure white privilege. Such goals include policies about taxation and social welfare programs that would disproportionately harm non-whites and, relatedly, benefit whites. Movements in which whiteness is an organizing principle need not be politically conservative, however. Organizations that are predicated upon anti-racism and upon attempts to subvert white privilege are also examples of whiteness mobilized.

Finally, Chapter 6 discusses the future of white racial identity. The demographic shifts that occur in America are likely to have profound implications on racial attitudes and identities. Whites (as currently defined) are soon to become a minority of the United States population; they are already a minority among the young population up to the age of 15 (Frey 2019). What will happen to whiteness when whites are no longer in the majority? Perhaps nothing—or perhaps there will be a strong shift in whites' attitudes and behaviors if they perceive their privileged position in society to be threatened. One form this may take would be for whites to draw even stronger boundaries around whiteness than the ones that currently exist. Such attempts could mirror and replicate, for instance, the behavior of native-born whites in America in the late nineteenth and early twentieth century, when waves of European immigrants from places such as Ireland and Italy were not considered fully "white." Alternatively, whites may erect weaker boundaries around their whiteness. In an attempt to maintain majority status, they may consider relabeling "white" groups that are currently "honorary whites," such as some Asians and Latinos/as. Finally, this chapter seeks to address the question: "Is there an ideal form of whiteness?" If a white individual were to care about the privilege and history of oppression that is associated with his or her identity, how might that person go about thinking and acting in ways that consciously challenge white privilege? While the connection between whiteness and privilege is not erasable, appreciating this connection and its many manifestations is a positive alternative to the passive acceptance of white racial dominance.

– 2 –

The Invisible Privilege of Whiteness

Learning about Race

Ideas about race and racial identity are learned early on. Psychologists have explored extensively the issue of racial identity development among children. Most of this research has been conducted with children of color—often black children—to assess the circumstances under which they perceive themselves as different from the white "norm." A number of these studies focus on the connection between racial awareness and perceptions of negative stereotypes. Perhaps the most famous one among them is that of the "doll test," originally conducted by Kenneth and Mamie Clark. Black and white children were shown two dolls, one white and one black, and were asked to pick the one they prefer. Black children chose the white doll, attributing positive characteristics such as "pretty" to it. White children also chose the white doll, recognizing the favored status of their own racial group (Powell-Hopson and Hopson 1988).

Psychological studies of racial identity carried out among white subjects typically find that the latter have difficulty articulating the characteristics of their racial identity. For example, Phinney's (1989) influential study of adolescent racial identity was unable to include the white students in the sample, as they mentioned no connection to a race at all, only to an "American" identity. Helms (1990) considered white racial identity as progressing through a series of stages, awareness of whiteness being one of the earliest stages in an ideal developmental process culminating in the acquisition of a non-racist white identity. In these stages, whites begin denying any information about race; they then become confused and question stereotypes; next, they respond to this confusion by asserting racial superiority; next, they recognize white racism; next, they try to find their own self-defined racial standards; finally, they adopt a complex analysis of racial material. Ultimately, according to this theory, the white individual has a healthy or positive understanding of his or her own racial identity (Mercer and Cunningham 2003).

Such stage models of the development of white racial identity have not been without their critics. Mercer and Cunningham (2003) argue for an approach that considers white identity as a coping mechanism for dealing with the stress of interracial interactions. The source of the stress may be cognitive dissonance, in which stereotypes and the reality of one's experience with individuals do not match. In order to deal with the stress, white identity may reflect either an adaptive or a maladaptive coping mechanism. White individuals may learn to be confident and comfortable in interracial interactions, or they form beliefs of inferiority and a desire to avoid such interactions in the future (Mercer and Cunningham 2003).

Learning about Race in the Family

One of the first sites of socialization is the family. It stands to reason, then, that many ideas about race are formed within families. For example, parental attitudes may be adopted directly, or parents may shape their children's belief systems. As with the psychological research on racial identity, much of the research on racial socialization within the family has focused on non-whites, especially blacks. This stands to reason, as blacks must navigate a hostile world that holds the potential for racial violence and discrimination without warning. Parents thus develop strategies to prepare their children for this reality as best they can. As white parents bear no such burden, the challenges they face in racially socializing their children pale by comparison. While white children receive many implicit messages from their parents about how to think about race, they typically receive fewer explicit ones (e.g. Lareau 2003).

Although the messages that white children receive about race in their families are not determinative of their racial attitudes—otherwise there would be no change in attitudes across generations—they can be influential (Sinclair, Dunn, and Lowery 2005). Much of what is known about these messages involve white attitudes toward non-whites; there have been very few studies of how white parents actively teach their children what it means to be *white*. Whiteness is an invisible, taken-for-granted norm against which the racialized other is juxtaposed. If race is discussed within the family, then, it is in the context of interacting with or judging a person of color rather than in a context of understanding how to carry oneself in the world as a white person. This stands in sharp contrast to the ways in which non-white children are socialized to be conscious of how their racial identity has the potential to influence every interaction they have.

Hagerman (2014, 2017, 2018) focuses specifically on the ways in which families socialize their children into whiteness. In her study of privileged white families, she finds that white racial identity is communicated more powerfully through actions than through words. Although some white parents had explicit conversations with their children about racial inequality—ranging from assertions of colorblindness (e.g. race doesn't matter anymore) to structural critiques—the choices and behaviors of parents had an even greater impact on their children. Affluent white parents make choices about where to live, where to send their children to school, and the kinds of activities for their children to participate in that create contexts for these children to learn about what it means to be white. For example, some of these children live around and socialize primarily with other whites, often seeing blacks as poor and dangerous others. One illustration of this process is the experience of privileged whites volunteering to help those in poverty. Some children absorb the lesson that to be black is to be underprivileged and that it is the duty of individual whites to help. This reinforces a conceptualization of whiteness as one of benevolent privilege begetting paternalism. On the other hand, some parents structure the volunteering experience for their children so that the latter see their privilege as connected to a larger racist system; their privilege is described as unearned and as existing at the expense of blacks, who are excluded from positions of power.

Some parents communicate explicitly with their children about race, although many do not. A study of white mothers found that its subjects neither communicated directly with their young children about race nor were able to accurately assess their children's racial attitudes (Pahlke et al. 2012). Some of the research finds that white parents who have non-white friendships tend to raise children with more progressive racial views, although there is no consensus among scholars that this is the case (Skinner and Meltzoff 2019). The transmission of racial attitudes from parents to children may occur in indirect ways, unobservable not only to the family members themselves but also to researchers using traditional survey instruments. Sinclair et al. (2005) have shown that racial prejudice can be transmitted *implicitly* rather than *explicitly* between parents and children, especially when children are highly identified with their parents. On the other hand, parents of very young children will sometimes communicate contempt for non-whites in ways that children not only absorb but deploy in the broader world (Van Ausdale and Feagin 2001). For example, some parents express fear of black men and stereotype them as violent criminals; their children then carry these beliefs with them, communicating them to their friends and enacting them in social life.

Racial attitudes and prejudice are conceptually distinct from white identity. The formation of racial identity critically involves not only the identification of oneself with a racial group, but also the continued differentiation between such groups. An important site for the early recognition of group boundaries and their maintenance is the school. In Amanda Lewis's (2003) *Race in the Schoolyard*, white students attending a majority-white suburban elementary school learn a colorblind ideology, absorbing lessons that race is neutral and that whiteness conveys no special advantages. They learn that racial categories exist, but to have a racial identity is thought to imply being a member of a non-white racial category. Perry (2002) finds more variance in white identity development at the high school level, where understandings of what it means to be white often differ for the same individual over time. Interactions with non-whites as well as the structure of their schools led students to think about their identity in both cultural and social terms. For example, tracking within schools meant that the perceived high-achieving, well-behaved students were in the all-white classrooms. Whiteness equaled goodness. One white student Perry interviewed made the following statement about some of the black and Latino/a students in her school: "When I see a twelfth grader holding a geometry book, I cringe inside me … people are so lazy, they don't care. They have no goals, no ambitions. It's frustrating! I don't get it!" (Perry 2001: 82). Without naming race, this student has learned to associate whiteness with achievement and industry.

White identity was sometimes considered consciously, and sometimes echoed Lewis's findings about colorblind ideology and the "neutrality" of whiteness. Bettie (2003)—in a study of a high school—finds that a group of working-class white students learned to associate overtly "white" symbols such as the Confederate flag with the assertive representation of their racial identity. Even though some of these students were not clear about the historical meaning of the flag, they nonetheless felt attached to it as a *racial* symbol (Bettie 2014: 172). However, it is not always the case that young people remain naïve about whiteness and white identity.

Whiteness Invisible

One of the most common findings in research on whiteness is its invisibility to those who possess it. For many whites, race refers only to blacks, Latinos/as, Asians, and American Indians. Whites, in effect, do not have a race—they are simply a default category. The invisibility of whiteness is pervasive in American society. Many whites go about their daily lives never thinking of themselves as having a race, which stands in sharp contrast to the way in which many non-whites must navigate everyday life. The "normal" state of affairs for whites is to live as if race played no role in their lives—anything else would be the result of an unusual encounter or event. In consequence, many whites fail to appreciate the everyday privileges that accrue to whiteness. For example, they are less likely to be followed in stores as shoplifting suspects (Henderson et al. 2016); they are less likely to be stopped by police (White 2015) and less likely to be given a ticket for a variety of minor infractions such as jaywalking (Soss and Weaver 2017); and they are more likely to be given a favorable mortgage loan (Ladd 1998; Massey et al. 2016). These advantages are directly predicated upon their white race, yet remain unseen. The absence of discriminatory treatment is hard to see. It is easy, however, to maintain a position of innocence when confronted with reports of discrimination or racism

(Levine-Rasky 2016)—if one didn't see it, it must have not happened.

Whiteness is often easiest to see when it is juxtaposed against another racial identity. White consciousness is thus more likely to manifest itself during interracial inter-actions, when whites are more likely to be aware of their racial difference. Whites who are isolated from non-whites—as is the case in many rural and suburban areas—have less opportunity to be reflective about their race, as their isolation enhances the association between being white and having "no race." Whether or not this awareness becomes a permanent part of whites' identity is an open question. Some research finds that interracial contact is the key to whites' greater awareness of their privileged position (Tropp and Barlow 2018), while others find that it has little impact on racial prejudice (Byrd 2014). White awareness is loosely connected to white attitudes and behavior.

The invisibility of white privilege to whites themselves is often called "colorblind racism" (Burke 2019). Colorblindness is the refusal to see racial difference; it often appears under the guise of seeing everyone as the same. One explains racial inequality by invoking individual differences rather than by making any reference to the consequences of a history of racism (Burke 2016). Some might say, "I don't see race. Everyone is just a human being," or "I don't care if you're black, red, blue, or purple." On the surface, these sound like admirable sentiments, as they imply not making negative judgments about those with racial identities different from one's own. However, this position of colorblindness is quite insidious, as the refusal to see racial differences results in an inability to acknowledge one's own racial privilege, or the degree of racial inequality in society. Hence the term colorblind *racism*: colorblindness actually results in greater rather than fewer invidious distinctions between racial groups, since those who espouse this position often see no need to address discrimination or oppression, as they have wished it out of existence. As a result, the distinctions between whites and blacks, for example, do not disappear—they grow even greater. It is nonetheless important to separate out colorblind *identity* from ideology, as do Hartmann et al. (2017). It is possible for colorblind goals to actually be important to an individual's self-image without being a part of a belief system that ignores racial discrimination (Burke 2019). The same individual may hold both egalitarian and unjust views simultaneously, as Knowles et al. (2009) find that exposing some individuals to threat can lead them to shift from believing that everyone should be treated equally to believing that nothing should be done about current inequalities. This is a common, real-world manifestation of colorblind racism: everyone is considered equal until policies or programs are suggested to give all racial groups equal opportunity; then the potential loss of white privilege is resisted and equality is redefined to mean invisibility.

One of the most influential descriptions of colorblind racism is by Eduardo Bonilla-Silva in *Racism without Racists: Color-Blind Racism and the Persistence of Racial Inequality in the United States* (Bonilla-Silva 2013). Bonilla-Silva outlines four key components of colorblind racism: abstract liberalism, naturalization, cultural racism, and minimization of racism. Abstract liberalism involves appeals to seemingly universal principles such as individualism (success should occur naturally, as a result of one's efforts) and equal opportunity (we all have the same chances in life). Naturalization refers to the ideas that whites use to justify racial inequality: that it unfolds "naturally," with no institutional or individual actors (segregated schools evolve naturally over time, for example). Cultural racism is, as the term suggests, a belief in the subordinate status of non-whites, owing to their common practices (these are often represented by stereotypes: e.g. blacks are more likely to be unemployed because they are lazy and don't want to work). The minimization of racism involves shrugging off current claims of racially disparate treatment and outcomes as minor; "real" racism occurred in the past, and racial inequality is not so bad now (overt, intended acts of discrimination are the only things that "count" as racism).

Bonilla-Silva's definition of colorblind racism encompasses many of the factors that render this set of beliefs about whiteness—and its presumed lack of a role in perpetuating racial inequality—so dangerous. When it is thought that racial privilege is a thing of the past and that racial inequality simply should not be discussed any longer, racial disparities persist while whites believe themselves to have no involvement in their existence. Not only do colorblind whites feel that they are not implicated in racist outcomes in America; they can actually feel virtuous at the same time (Stoll and Klein 2018). For instance, claiming that all people are equal and that one "doesn't see race" sounds like a noble position. Yet not seeing race involves not acknowledging one's own race and the privilege it entails. To be racially invisible is to disown responsibility for racial injustice, especially if one assumes that only extreme, violent words or acts toward non-whites count as racism.

Individualism is a component of abstract liberalism that is also a foundation of colorblindness. Whites who think of themselves merely as individuals and not as members of a race are much less likely to recognize the existence of racism. In order for racism to exist, in this way of thinking, an individual white person would have to independently engage in a conscious action of discriminating against or otherwise harming a person of color. In addition, the achievements (or lack thereof) of an individual would be solely the result of their actions, not the result of structural advantages or roadblocks. Thus a white valedictorian might consider his or her achievements the result of intelligence and hard work, while thinking that the poor academic performance of a black classmate was due to a lack of those qualities. The large number of other factors potentially responsible for the discrepancy, such as different academic opportunities (Solórzano and Ornelas 2002), different degrees of assistance inside and outside school (Englund et al. 2004), and the impact of stereotypes (Zirkel 2005) would not enter the awareness of the white student who is rooted in an ideology of individualism.

The naturalization of racism that Bonilla-Silva describes refers to the belief that racial differences "just happen," or seem magically to unfold without anyone or anything taking an action. Whites who claim that racial differences in social outcomes are just the way things are underestimate the significant role that individuals and institutions play in generating racial inequality. Observing that there happen to be "black neighborhoods" and "white neighborhoods" without considering how segregated neighborhoods came about is an example of the naturalization of racism. Discriminatory home-lending practices and the violent intimidation of non-whites who try to move into majority white neighborhoods are some of the reasons why residential segregation exists; it is not a natural phenomenon (Rothstein 2017; Bell 2013). Taking its existence for granted and believing it to be part of the natural order of things might seem innocent enough, but this kind of attitude maintains a sense of white privilege by denying any role of racist actions taken by whites or white-controlled organizations in creating inequality. Thus whites' residence in neighborhoods with lower crime rates and higher achieving schools can be seen as their natural right rather than as occurring at the cost of others' opportunities.

Cultural racism is another means by which whites may ignore their racial advantages. To cultural racists, people of color bring their struggles upon themselves through their own practices. For example, whites who rail against the style of dress or cadence of speech of blacks might assert that these are the reasons for blacks' high rate of unemployment. Assumptions that it is the choices that non-whites make that are responsible for racial inequality rather than the discrimination that they face allow whites to distance themselves from any responsibility for their own actions. Whiteness is the neutral default, while non-whites' behavior and attitudes are conceptualized as deviant. As will be seen in Chapter 4, this conceptualization is linked to support for a punitive criminal justice system as well as to opposition to a variety of social welfare programs.

Finally, the minimization of racism enables whites to erase the distance between the experiences and opportunities of different racial groups and those of their own group by asserting that contemporary experiences of racism are simply "not that bad." Arguments in favor of policy measures designed to ameliorate racial equality might be opposed by claiming that the *real* racial problems were connected to slavery (or Jim Crow) and that nothing less than systems of systematic racial terror should be taken seriously. As a corollary, whites who minimize racial inequality also distance themselves from slavery and enforced segregation, noting that they (and in some cases their ancestors) were not present when these abuses took place, and therefore they bear no responsibility for any present-day racial inequality. Yet again, whiteness is detached from its role in creating and maintaining discrimination.

All these components of colorblindness have one thing in common: the desire to deny the reality of white privilege. By simply not talking about race in any way, whites can ignore racial difference; and, if they ignore racial difference, they need not look to their own role in perpetuating this difference. Colorblindness—not seeing color—sounds like an ideal position. Indeed, many argue that this should be our ultimate societal goal. However, at this moment in history, not seeing color means not seeing one's own group privilege; and this is a position that instead perpetuates inequality. Acknowledging and discussing racial difference, not just non-white disadvantage but also white advantage, is the path toward equality.

Hegemonic Whiteness

Colorblindness exists because of the ways in which whiteness is embedded in every institution in America. Several sociologists have written about this enmeshment, calling it "hegemonic whiteness" or "hegemonic racism." Hegemony refers to the totalizing dominance of an organization or phenomenon over everything in its sphere of possible influence, often with the consent of the disadvantaged (Gramsci 1971). For example, colonizing states have been referred to as "hegemons," as they exercise total dominion over the countries they control. The forms of control can vary by race; thus working-class whites may be offered concessions from the state that are not available to non-whites (Arena 2003). White workers might then support an economic system that functions against their own interests; those who exploit the workers need not coerce them into accepting lower wages, for example, as the workers willingly accept their position (Artz and Murphy 2000). One powerful way in which white workers (and women, and other marginalized groups) accept a system that exploits them is by embracing the ideology of whiteness. Whiteness can serve as a kind of concession, insuring the loyalty of those who are disadvantaged by the economic practices of the overarching structure. Whiteness can also be thought of as a form of hegemonic control, white privilege working its way into every aspect of social life. As with colorblindness, the extent of this privilege is often invisible. Not only white advantage is not realized; so, too, is the way in which "white" is assumed to be the standard across a range of institutions and practices. The white perspective that permeates American institutions is not simply a matter of numbers—of whites being more likely to be represented in these institutions. It is also built into the rules of these institutions and into the actions they take.

The hegemonic dominance of whiteness is so powerful that it may actually kill some of the white people who accept it. The lower life expectancies among blacks noted in Chapter 1 are, in part, a result of discrimination. Although whites do not face racial discrimination, within the white population there are differences in life expectancy that are based on class and gender. Case and Deaton (2015) document declining life expectancies for middle-aged white Americans over the last two decades, and the decline is sharper for less educated whites. The cause is thought to be "diseases of despair" such as suicide, drug overdoses, and liver disease related to alcoholism. Even though whites still have health advantages over blacks, they nonetheless are subject to economic pressures and to a lack of social services, all of which increase the risk for self-inflicted death. Ironically, many whites resist measures that would very likely increase their life expectancies. For example, Metzl (2019) finds that whites in Missouri and Tennessee actively oppose gun control (which would reduce suicides) and the Affordable Care Act (which facilitates the provision of medical and psychological services). Metzl argues that the main reason why whites oppose policies that would improve their health and well-being is racial resentment. Their support for policies packaged as part of a plan to maintain white dominance—or white hegemony—leads them to vote or argue against their own interests. Metzl (2019: 9) writes that "white America's investment in maintaining an imagined place atop a racial hierarchy—that is, an investment in a sense of whiteness—ironically harms the aggregate well-being of US whites as a demographic group, thereby making whiteness itself a negative health indicator." In other words, the hegemony of whiteness leads to the consent of whites to be exploited politically … sometimes at the cost of their lives.

Hegemonic whiteness is so powerful not only because it permeates all parts of daily life, but also because it goes almost completely unnoticed. By virtue of the structural nature of white privilege, the degree to which institutions embody it is non-obvious in a way in which the presence of racial themes in interracial interactions is not. While whites may intentionally overlook racial inequality as it is manifest in obvious differences in social outcomes or in the tenor of interracial interactions, whites' overlooking the *structure* of white privilege can be wholly unintentional, as it is part of the taken-for-granted nature of American life. For example, the ability of whites to exist in social spaces without being under a cloud of suspicion, or the greater access to mortgage loans that many whites have (Ladd 1998; Massey et al. 2016), are taken for granted. They are not counterpoised to the suspicion that non-whites experience or to the difficulty that non-whites have in securing a loan.

Amanda Lewis (2004) discusses hegemonic whiteness in terms of its ideological power. The beliefs and practices associated with whiteness that support the status quo of racial inequality are engaged in without reflection. She is careful to note, however, that the experience of hegemonic whiteness is not likely to be the same for all whites; their structural position makes a difference. She writes: "Whiteness works in distinct ways and is embodied quite differently by homeless white men, golf-club-membership-owning executives, suburban soccer moms, urban hillbillies, antiracist skinheads, and/or union-card-carrying factory workers" (Lewis 2004: 634). As whiteness itself is connected to social structures, it stands to reason that the ways in which practices and ideas associated with it vary are based on the structural location of whites. The corporate executive might feel that privilege and power are the necessary desserts of whiteness, while the homeless person might confront white privilege less directly (although perhaps still being relatively protected from police by comparison to his or her non-white counterparts).

Research on the ways in which factors such as class and gender interact with whiteness reflect a concern with intersectionality. Intersectional approaches have long been practiced in sociology and related disciplines, but contemporary theories of intersectionality emerged from the black feminist movement. Crenshaw (1989) identifies the ways in which being both black and female can result in outcomes that are different from those that would result from race or class alone. For example, black women who are treated unfairly at work by comparison to both black men *and* white women would be unable to file a discrimination lawsuit based on either gender or race discrimination, since black men are being treated relatively fairly (hence no documented race discrimination) and white women are also being treated relatively fairly (hence no gender discrimination). Romero (2018) contrasts the experiences of gay Latino/a parents who wish to volunteer at their daughter's school with the experience of a straight white working poor woman who is single, also wishing to volunteer at her daughter's school. Each of these people experiences different forms of oppression and privilege—the example Romero provides would be thought about differently if the comparison were simply between whites and Latinos/as. Arguments and studies such as these are of direct relevance to the study of whiteness. There are many different ways in which whiteness—and especially white identity—is understood and expressed, depending on the other identities that intersect with "white."

Factors such as class and gender can lead to conflicts among whites themselves about the meanings of whiteness (Wray 2019). Authors such as Wray claim that "the benefits of white skin privilege are scarce to non-existent for whites on the lower rungs of the social ladder" (2019: 39). It can be difficult to be reflective about white privilege when reading about the rates of sexual violence or wage discrimination against women. Likewise, discrimination against white members of the LGBTQ community and restricted opportunities for disabled white Americans can make it difficult to see the ways in which these categories reap the benefits of whiteness. Some whites who have converted to Islam actually experience islamophobia—a seeming forfeiture of their white privilege (Galonnier 2015), although their structural position in life at the time of conversion had been a result of their benefitting from their whiteness.

Perhaps what is most important is the extent to which members of these groups—those who have marginalized statuses that *intersect* with the dominant status of being white—see themselves as either benefitting from being white or as having had these benefits cancelled out. Is it the case, as Wray wrote, that the benefits of white privilege are *non-existent* for whites with cross-cutting marginalized statuses such as poverty, or are the benefits just more complicated? It is certainly possible to think about the advantages of whiteness as residing in structural benefits that don't simply involve greater wealth or freedom from discrimination. If having a marginalized status leads to the recognition of the experience of discrimination, yet the individual can have a simultaneous awareness of white privilege that prevents him or her from failing to recognize the ways in which he or she is structurally advantaged, a more thoughtful appreciation of the effects of racial inequality may emerge. For instance, there is some evidence that LGB whites are less likely to endorse racism than their heterosexual counterparts (Grollman 2018).

Ultimately, the ideologies and practices of whiteness invisibly pervade the lives of all whites. Lewis argues that there is a single dominant form of hegemonic whiteness in any given time period; and it is this form that supports the existence of white supremacy. Importantly, hegemonic whiteness is collective in nature, even as individuals may experience it differently. It is the pursuit of the ideal form of white identity that holds disparate whites together, not just their structural advantages (Hughey and Byrd 2013). In this way, an impoverished white person experiences whiteness just as a wealthy person does.

Hughey (2010) has conceived of hegemonic whiteness specifically in terms of white racial identity. While it is tempting to focus on the ways in which white people think differently about what it means to be white, he argues that there is ultimately one material reality underlying each form of identity. In his study of a white nationalist organization and a white anti-racist organization comprised primarily of men, he notices a striking similarity in the ways in which members of the disparate groups conceive of whiteness. In particular, both groups of whites reify differences (and white superiority) between whites and non-whites, and both groups of whites "marginaliz(e) practices of 'being white' that fail to exemplify dominant ideals" (Hughey 2010: 1290). Hence there is a "hegemonic" form of whiteness that all whites expect conformity with; and this form implies the superior position of whites. According to Hughey, these understandings of white identity are not a product of inhabiting a particular social context, but are instead reflections of racial ideologies that are dominant throughout society.

The hegemony of whiteness is also manifest in the existence of certain sports mascots. Native American mascots have been criticized as offensive to members of indigenous groups. For many years, such mascots were a virtually unquestioned part of community life throughout America. The degree to which these mascots put forward an image of Native Americans as violent or "savage" went unnoticed by whites, who cheered them on. When opposition to such mascots emerged, it was met with a serious backlash. As previously unquestioned white privilege came to be questioned, defenders of the mascots discussed how these objects symbolized their identities and were conduits for the investment of their emotions (Callais 2010). These supporters thought of themselves as "sports fans," not as whites. In this case, the hegemony of whiteness extends even to the seemingly race-neutral arena of sports fandom.

The influence of whiteness throughout institutions can lead to practices that seem like common-sense—even, in some cases, to non-whites; and yet these practices reinforce white hegemony. Flores (2016) provides an example of this influence by analyzing the dominant form of bilingual education, "liberal multiculturalism." This idea of bilingual education as a tool for helping non-native English-speaking children develop their English-speaking abilities has widespread support. What could possibly be the harm in teaching, for example, Latino/a children how to speak the language most commonly used in the United States? While there may be no direct harm, the development of bilingual education programs has emphasized their importance as a means to enhance the skills of native English speakers, who are often white. The learning of a second language is considered an asset in these children's higher education and their careers; at the same time Latinos/as are corrected if they codeswitch between Spanish and English, as many do in their communities (Flores 2016). Ultimately, Latinos/as are criticized and white students rewarded, all as part of a program developed to enrich everyone. The vast majority of the people who design and implement such programs are well intentioned, yet whites ultimately benefit. This is hegemonic whiteness at work.

It may sound strange to think of something as important as white racial identity as being invisible, yet this has been the dominant feature of whiteness throughout contemporary American history. Whiteness has been thought of as the neutral, default category against which all other racial groups are compared. Most whites never think about having a race at all, and many believe that races should not even exist. Yet all whites are forced by the practicalities of bureaucratic life to use a particular term to refer to their own race, even if that term is simply "none of the above." Martin et al. (1999) find that the majority of whites prefer the term "white" as a label that describes their racial identity, "Caucasian" being the second most popular term. There was little variation in label preference according to the demographic characteristics of the respondents. Most of those in the study were unable to provide sensible definitions of whiteness—they would respond with comments such as "white means white," suggesting that there isn't a meaningful sense of one's identity for most whites (Martin et al. 1999). Doane (1997a) sees this self-labeling as merely "white" as indicative of a merging of racial and ethnic identities. No longer "WASP" (white Anglo-Saxon Protestant) or "European origin group," the designation "white" now divorces identity from its historical origins. This "may give rise to attempts to divorce whiteness from its historical legacy of oppression and privilege and to recast it as simply another identity" (Doane 1997a: 389). There are consequences to this invisibility of race: if whiteness is not recognized, the powerful, pervasive effects of white privilege risk going unnoticed. At the same time, asserting that society should not care about race at all risks overlooking the many instances of racial discrimination in America. "Colorblindness" is not only a common position of whites, it is also a major ideological support for racism in the US. Colorblindness will be a recurring theme throughout the book, as it shapes Americans' beliefs about politics and social issues (Chapter 4), in addition to serving as the basis for social movements that are implicitly organized around goals that benefit whites (Chapter 5).

– 3 –
Whiteness Visible

Although whiteness is often invisible to those who possess it, being assumed to be the default, "normal" racial category, white identity is not always hidden from those who have it. While the colorblindness described in the previous chapter is a dominant form of whiteness today, it is not always the case that whites minimize their racial identities. For example, Hartmann et al. (2009) and Jardina (2019) find that a substantial proportion of whites believe that their white identity is important to them. In general, Southerners and people with lower levels of education are most likely to embrace their whiteness. At the same time, men and people who identified as Republican were much less likely to see a connection between whiteness and privilege (Hartmann et al. 2009). People who identify strongly with whiteness appear at both ends of the political spectrum—among the most as well as among the least progressive (Croll 2007; Jardina 2019).

Whites who are acutely conscious of their whiteness typically express this in one of three ways, each with its own origins and its own consequences for behavior. When whites are considered to have fallen short of the expectations generated by white privilege, they are looked down upon for being white; in such cases whiteness is experienced as "stigma." It is visible, to themselves and to others, as a mark of the failure to live up to the expectation that white members of society be economically successful. Next, whiteness can also be "defensive" when whites feel under attack from non-whites, whom they perceive as taking "their" resources—for example the schools their children attend, or the jobs they feel they have a right to. As a result of such feelings, they have heightened awareness of their whiteness as a source of rights and privilege. Finally, whiteness can be "transcendent" when whites who are hyperaware of their white identity try to escape it, often by adopting a non-white identity (McDermott 2010). It is not the case that whites who fit into any of these categories do not also experience colorblind racism, but their perspectives are not completely dominated by it. Whites in any of these three groups may subscribe to some of the beliefs associated with colorblind racism, but their perspectives of all of them are at least in some ways color-sensitive.

Stigma

The term "stigma" describes the negative effect of prejudice on the marginalized group or individual whom that prejudice targets. For instance, much has been written about the stigma of being mentally ill. Many people have negative stereotypes about the mentally ill and practice distancing from or discriminating against them (Markowitz 2005). Hence mental illness has its own stigma—a status that carries with it the marginalizing effects of prejudice.

Perhaps the most well-known scholar to write about stigma was Erving Goffman (1963). Goffman wrote about people whose attributes lead others to dissociate themselves from them. For example, he considers people with a physical disfigurement, who are regarded as falling outside what is considered normal for society. In his view, the dynamic of stigma results from relationships between attributes such as being poor and stereotypes such as being lazy. Impoverished people would thus be stigmatized as lazy.

Over the years, after Goffman's initial publications, many social scientists have further developed the concept of stigma. In an extensive review of the literature, Link and Phelan (2001) identify five key components to this phenomenon. People initially "distinguish and label differences" (2001: 367), then connect these labels with negative stereotypes. The stereotyped group is then categorized; the purpose is that we may distinguish "them" from "us." The resulting loss of status for the stigmatized group leads to their doing worse than the non-stigmatized group in a variety of ways. The entire process of stigmatization depends upon the stigmatizers' ability to apply labels and stereotypes. The application of stereotypes to groups, with a resultant loss of status, is not possible if the group applying the stereotypes is in a subordinate position.

The dominant group often feels threatened in some way by the subordinate group. This is easy to see, for example, in the case of contagious diseases, where the healthy (the dominant group) feel physically threatened by the ill (the subordinate group). However, the threat need not be so literal. Symbolic threat can be just as important in generating stigma. This is especially true when a group's value system has been violated (Stangor and Crandall 2000); for example, when heterosexuals feel that gays or lesbians threaten the moral sanctity of their own group. Such threats can "pose a threat to the vitality of the individual or the culture" (2000: 74). This conceptualization of threat and stigma as symbolic opens up the possibility for one group of whites to stigmatize another group of whites, as one group of whites may have characteristics (such as poverty) that threaten the representative power of whiteness.

The process of stigmatization does not occur in a vacuum. The local context in which the stigmatized and the stigmatizers are embedded plays an important role in shaping conceptions of group attributes. It has been argued that the question of what beliefs and behaviors are "correct" in a particular setting or moral context is especially important for the development of stigma (Kleinman and Hall-Clifford 2009). While there may be generalizable attributes (such as poverty) associated with a stigmatized group, the effect of these attributes on dominant group perceptions will be conditioned by the local context (Kleinman and Hall-Clifford 2009). In addition, the characteristics of the situational context (i.e. the setting in which people are talking to one another) can cause a characteristic to be stigmatized in one set of inter- actions but not in another (Dovidio, Major, and Crocker 2000). Context powerfully shapes the different ways in which whites—as members of a dominant group—can experience stigma on the basis of their race.

As stigma always characterizes the outsider group, it can be difficult to imagine how dominant group status gets to be stigmatized. While members of dominant groups may experience stigma for many reasons—numerous white men suffer from mental illness, for example—there are cases in which it is the status of whiteness *itself* that is stigmatized. One especially prominent case is that of white poverty. While poverty is almost always stigmatized (Fiske 2011), the combination of being poor and being white leads to an even greater stigmatization. The dominant racial status is in effect polluted for poor whites.

As mentioned previously, theories of intersectionality predict that the combination of different statuses—or social locations—may result in outcomes that are not simply additive (Collins 2015). Being a black female is not equivalent with having the experience of being black and having the experience of being a woman happen indepen- dently. There is rather a unique experience attached to this kind of combination of identities. This is especially true when one identity is dominant and the other is subor- dinate, since the two don't merely cancel each other out;

they shape the beliefs and experiences of those who fall in the two categories, and they do so in ways that cannot be predicted from membership of just one of them. Just as whites do not experience their racial privilege in the same way, poor people of different races have different courses through life. Depending on how one thinks about different identities intersecting, one aspect of experience will be highlighted in relation to another; for example, one might be thought of as a privileged poor person or as a disadvantaged white person. Intersectional theory suggests that neither of these ways of thinking about people in multiple categories is correct, since the identities operate jointly and generate particular practices and understandings.

The combination of a privileged racial status and a subordinate economic status results in a form of pollution of the privileged status: poor whites can be seen as having forfeited, presumably through their own actions, the benefits to which they were entitled. This assumption generates a series of denigrations, such as the ones embodied in the term "white trash." White trash, used as a synonym for poor whites, designates especially the low status of this group—they are deemed subhuman, hence "trash," while at the same time they are noted, importantly, to be white. The label is sometimes used with the intent of shaming and demonizing an entire set of cultural practices (Hartigan Jr. 2003).

In the United States, the stigmatization of whiteness when associated with poverty is built upon the stereotype that non-whites necessarily are a lower class and inhabit a lower status (Gilens 1996). In popular culture, poor Americans are often represented as people of color, and the portrayal of poor people in political discussions uses the same imagery. And yet, while rates of poverty are indeed high among non-white groups (with the exception of Asian Americans), it is nonetheless the case that many blacks, Latinos/as, and American Indians are of middle-class status and that the number of people living in poverty is higher among whites than among members of any other racial group. But this factual reality has not decoupled either the associations between race and socioeconomic status or the corresponding stereotypes that pair up whiteness and wealth, blackness and poverty. As a result, in America it looks as if poor whites would subvert a "natural" hierarchy, generating discomfort and opprobrium in the larger society outside their group—and sometimes self-loathing in their own ranks.

One curious aspect of the stigmatization of poor whites is the degree to which broad swaths of society find it acceptable to engage in shows of disdain and mockery for this group. Even educated elites make fun of the presumed cultural attributes of "white trash"—when they would not ridicule many other groups in society. There is no need to add a class specifier like "trash" to names such as "black" or "Latino/a," since a racist notion is implicit in the use of the racial term itself (Newitz and Wray 1997).

By their very existence, poor whites highlight the taken-for-granted nature of privilege that resides in whiteness. When the economic benefits of this privilege are not forthcoming, those who *do* reap them comfortably may feel uncomfortable. It is this discomfort that expresses itself in jokes and ridicule directed at poor whites. Since whiteness is expected to confer automatic economic benefits, those without such benefits are thought to be defective in some way. For example, they are assumed to be ignorant, lacking in family values, loud, or even prone to criminal behavior (Webster 2008). While there are plenty of stereotypes that blame poor non-white individuals for their socioeconomic standing, there is a particularly widespread sense that poor whites have no one but themselves to blame for struggling to make ends meet, since they were born with the advantage of a white skin. Sometimes these whites are blamed for failing to work hard enough; other times they are blamed for failing to live up to the moral standards of whiteness, standards such as having a small family, or avoiding drug use and excessive alcohol consumption.

While the stigmatization of whiteness can be seen most clearly in the case of poor whites, working-class whites, too, are sometimes considered not to live up to the privileges of whiteness. If being white means being educated and affluent, working-class people fall short. Middle-class and elite whites have mobilized a host of negative stereotypes that emphasize the supposed ignorance of working-class whites (Williams 2017). These include beliefs that the latter are intolerant, unintelligent, provincial, and unable to act in their own interests. Such beliefs about the working class are pervasive enough to have penetrated public consciousness, even if, to be sure, not all socioeconomically privileged whites share them.

Major and O'Brien (2005) outline three main ways in which stigmatized groups may respond to the negative attitudes and treatment they receive. One is to shift the blame from the individual to the group. In the case of poor or working-class whites, this would mean viewing the insults they receive as a result of anti-class bias rather than as a result of their own failures to live up to their promise in life. Since the discourse around class inequality in America is a muted one, this is an unlikely response to stigma among poor whites. A second strategy that Major and O'Brien describe is for the group to disengage from the behaviors that are most stigmatized, as do women who avoid math questions on an exam. Since the stigmatization of whiteness in interaction with class is so broadly applied, it is difficult to see how this strategy might work. The final strategy presented by Major and O'Brien consists in greater group identification or disidentification. Poor whites might distance themselves from their racial identity entirely, perhaps seeking an alternative one. Conversely, poor and working-class whites might develop an even stronger race or class consciousness in response to being critiqued for not being good enough as far as both race and class go. This final strategy may have been employed by some working-class whites during the 2016 presidential election.

In addition, stigmatized individuals might reduce the impact of negative feedback (Barreto 2015). Poor whites might avoid comparing themselves to others—for example, to middle-class whites. They may also try to hide their identity or, conversely, to confront those who express prejudice against them (Barreto 2015). Such confrontations are not often reported, although one might argue that the anti-elite strain in American politics is a reflection of that kind of confrontation.

Miller and Kaiser (2001) identify other strategies of stigma avoidance. One of them involves cognitive restructuring, whereby the thinking of the stigmatized individual changes so as to provide a positive framing for that person's position in the world. A good example of cognitive restructuring is a white restaurant server who reported being looked down upon because of her job. She said:

> When I was a server I was embarrassed to say I was a server. ... And it took me a long time to be proud that I worked there. And then I realized, I don't ask anyone for anything. I pay all my own bills, I take care of my child. Everything that I have, I've worked for. I don't ask anyone for anything, so why am I ashamed to say where I work? (McDermott et al. 2019)

Although this woman felt stigmatized because she was a white person with a working-class job, she was able to reframe her position so as to attribute positive individual qualities to herself.

Working-class whites have long perceived the elite's contempt for them. Arguably these perceptions have had significant political implications for quite some time. The contempt was never more clearly emphasized than in the 2016 US presidential election, when many white working-class voters shifted their support from Democrats to Republicans. While there were no doubt many reasons behind this shift, one that was repeated in journalists' interviews with working-class white voters and capitalized upon by Donald Trump was the supposed contempt for working-class whites expressed by Hillary Clinton and, by extension, other elites. Clinton's famous assertion in a speech that a racist half of Trump's supporters belonged in a "basket of deplorables" was declared by Trump to be an aspersion cast on working people. Working-class voters were consequently angered by their perceived stigmatization as stereotypical working-class whites—as racist members of a "deplorable" outgroup. This prompted them to support wholeheartedly the candidate perceived to demonstrate respect for their group. That said, working-class whites *are* much more likely to have anti-immigrant attitudes than are college educated whites (Gest 2016). Nonetheless, middle-class and elite whites are people with the actual resources to facilitate the implementation of anti-immigrant policies—or at least to help shift whites' beliefs about immigrants and non-whites (Spanierman, Garriott, and Clark 2013).

After Donald Trump's victory in the 2016 election, the stigmatization of working-class whites by elites has only escalated. The stereotype of ignorant working-class whites was capitalized upon to bemoan the fact that this underprivileged group had acted against its own interest by electing a politician who would enact policies directly at odds with its economic well-being. Even though approximately a third of working-class whites voted for Clinton, the group as a whole was treated by some white elites as largely responsible for Trump's victory and as having disowned the sophisticated and thoughtful mantle of whiteness that should have been its members' birthright. At the same time, many working-class white voters—joined by a number from the middle-classes—capitalized upon their white privilege by asserting strongly nativist positions. Overt racism is sometimes associated with poor and working-class whites—especially with the "rednecks" from the rural south. This is a way elite whites can distance themselves from their own racial prejudice: they place the responsibility for such beliefs on less economically privileged whites (Hardie and Tyson 2013).

There are very few conditions in which stigma can be attached to the dominant category of white, and the combination of whiteness with poverty is one of them. When whites—members of a highly privileged and often affluent group—are not aware of their middle- or upper-class status and of the advantages it brings, it is often assumed that individual flaws are the root cause of financial setbacks. This, in turn, results in those who are both poor and white bearing a special stigma, since they have failed to achieve what was allegedly a given. At least one case demonstrates, however, that the stigmatization of whites occurs even when they have an upper-middle class status, yet still have failed to achieve what is expected of whites. Jiménez and Horowitz (2013) interviewed whites and Asian Americans from an affluent suburb in Northern California, where high schools produce highly successful students who go on to attend a range of top-ranked colleges. In this competitive environment, it is *white* students who are thought of as not very smart, despite having the privilege of belonging to the racially dominant group in America. One of the respondents in this study says: "It was always interesting battling the stereotype of white people aren't as driven, they're not quite as smart" (Jiménez and Horowitz 2013: 860). Any failure to be the very best is a subversion of the expectations of the dominant group and can lead to a degree of stigmatization.

Class status is not the only characteristic that combines with whiteness to produce a special form of stigmatization of a dominant category. The neighborhood or region in which individuals reside can also taint the privileged status of whiteness in much the same way as does poverty. If one were living up to the status of being white and its corollary positive stereotypes of affluence, power and mastery, one would not live in such places as trailer parks or economically depressed urban neighborhoods near non-whites. Certain subregions of the United States, such as Middle and Southern Appalachia, also carry a stigma for the whites who live in them—a stigma over and above the degree of poverty that is prevalent there. To a lesser extent, for whites, residence in the southern parts of the United States carries a stigma that it does not carry for non-whites (Shirley 2010). An increasing rural–urban divide in America has generated a greater stigmatization of rural whites than has existed in the past. Morris (2012) finds that working-class whites living in a rural community with a declining economy are quite aware of the negative stereotypes that those in the rest of the country hold about them, considering them ignorant and backward. However, the whites he studied embraced the terms "redneck" and "hillbilly," which are normally meant to convey condescension and contempt, and used them instead as badges of honor, deploying them as symbols of hard work (Morris 2012). This contrasts with the treatment of the term "white trash," which is embraced with pride only by very few (Hartigan Jr. 2003). This term (with its local variants) is used to demarcate the poorest of whites and to create clear boundaries between those who are morally righteous and those who are unclean and unworthy, thus preventing the spread of the "contagion" of bad hygiene and poor values to whites whose social class aligns with their whiteness (Morris 2012).

The American South has been stereotyped as a place with many poor whites; in consequence, impoverished whites in this part of the country are, in some respects, doubly stigmatized. In order to explore some of the dynamics of the perceptions around white poverty in this part of the country, Shirley (2010) interviewed whites from rural Mississippi about their views on race and class. Most respondents were aware of non-southerners' negative stereotypes about southerners. More affluent respondents who spent time living outside their local communities were especially likely to believe that outsiders thought of them as racially prejudiced, while lower class interviewees were more likely to believe that the rest of the world viewed them as rednecks. Higher status interviewees were especially likely to draw distinctions between rednecks and white trash. One woman whom Shirley interviewed stated:

> To me there is a difference between dirty dirt and clean dirt. You have a man come in here who's worked all day. He's hot and sweaty, that to me is honest, clean dirt. You have others who come in here whose hands are so filthy you know they haven't washed them in god knows when. You can see the dirt on their neck, you can see their hair hanging in clumps. That's not like going out and working all day. (Shirley 2010: 51)

To this woman, the dirt of the poorest white person actually darkens that person's skin to a greater extent than the "cleaner" dirt of the hard-working white person.

The people whom Shirley's interviewees label "white trash" are often stereotyped as living in trailer parks. In the United States, 7 percent of all housing units are mobile homes (ACS 2005). They are concentrated in southern states such as South Carolina (18.5 percent) and Mississippi (15.7 percent), as well as in relatively rural states in the west such as New Mexico (17.8 percent) and Wyoming (14.8 percent). Eighty-one percent of mobile home residents are white (Foremost Insurance Group n.d.); even though only about a half of the mobile homes are located in trailer parks, the overall racial composition is likely to be similar. In addition, residents of mobile home parks are likely to have low incomes and relatively low levels of education. The demographics of the trailer park make it a symbol of the stigmatized category of white poverty—a stereo-typed space of laziness, violence, and moral turpitude that bears the brunt of middle-class and elite judgment, cast upon poor whites who have not fully realized the potential of their inherent privilege. Trailer parks are not only associated with white poverty (Moss 2003), they are also a challenge to assumptions about where whites are supposed to live. Single-family suburban homes or spotless townhouses in the city are common representations of white residences; small, less well-constructed homes in densely populated developments in less desirable parts of rural and suburban communities challenge these assumptions. Although trailer parks are not in fact more likely to be sites of crime than are other low-income communities (Barthe et al. 2014), images of trailer parks as locations of drug dealing and violence are persistent.

Residents of trailer parks are very much aware of the stigma attached to living in them. They have declared that they acknowledge they live on the "other side of the tracks" and would avoid telling others where they live (MacTavish 2006). One young person interviewed by MacTavish in a rural trailer park said:

> It was like I was assumed to be stupid. Like when the teacher hands back papers and says there were so many A's and so many B's. Everyone tries to guess who the A's are. They never think it could be me. Even when I say I got an A, they're like, "No—it couldn't be you." ... When I walk down the hall, the way I get hailed, the kids call out "Hey Trailer Trash." I'm good at blocking things out though. I hardly hear it anymore. (MacTavish 2006: 12–13)

One of the privileges of whiteness is the assumption of intelligence. In many racially integrated schools, it is white students who are assumed to be A students and non-white students who are thought to be "stupid." But the stigmatization of both class and place have changed the meaning of whiteness for some. It still confers privileges, but those privileges are not experienced unambiguously, in the same way as they are for whites whose class and residence match racialized expectations.

Whites who receive the sobriquet "trailer trash" have developed multiple strategies for dealing with the stigma attached to it (Kusenbach 2009). The strategy most commonly adopted by Kusenbach's interviewees from a trailer park in Florida is distancing. They articulate the ways in which they are very different from—better than—the other whites who live in trailers, for example through moral superiority or through the superior condition of their homes. Similarly, Moss (2003) finds that residents of trailer parks in the Midwest make distinctions among themselves based on owning versus renting, or on the size of the trailer. For these low-income whites, living in a trailer was *not* a mark of failing to live up to the privileges of whiteness, as it might seem to outsiders.

Southern cities such as Atlanta and Midwestern cities such as Detroit had distinctive neighborhoods of poor whites, who are stigmatized not merely for their poverty but also for their address (Hartigan 1999; McDermott 2006). This socio-spatial stigmatization is similar to that of trailer parks (Sullivan 2018), although the stigma that whites experience in these neighborhoods is not generated by the type of housing, but rather by its relative location. Because of the proximity of these neighborhoods to majority black neighborhoods, whites living in these locations are especially stigmatized: "real" whites would have moved up and out by now, away from non-whites. Many of the whites who settled in these now vanishing urban enclaves were "hillbillies" who migrated out of Appalachia and other rural communities of the South in search of employment in the expanding economies of cities. Their speech and dress immediately set them apart from the existing white residents, who quickly placed social as well as physical distance between themselves and the newcomers. Their residence near predominantly black communities ensured that the initial stigma attached to their distinctive character persisted even as other working-class and middle-class whites moved out of the city and to the suburbs. In recent years these poor white urban communities have been slowly disappearing, being replaced in some places by majority African American neighborhoods and in others by white gentrifiers—who wear their racial privilege publicly and unambiguously as affluent urbanites.

While class, neighborhood, and region are macro-level factors that can render whiteness a stigmatized category, micro-level phenomena can also play a role. For example, whites who married non-whites—especially whites who married African Americans—could suffer a significant loss in status by virtue of choosing to live as an equal with someone who is not white (Rosenthal et al. 2019). This act of becoming a "traitor" to the white race—an accusation white racists might hurl at people who get involved in interracial relationships (as well as at people who get involved in fights for racial justice)—is so stigmatizing to the white partner in the relationship that such partners could be shunned by their family and community. As in the other examples of whiteness being stigmatized, the negative status of white persons is predicated upon the anti-black racism that undergirds America. This racism seeks to maintain boundaries between blacks and whites, and the boundaries—especially in the area of sex—are so rigid that any significant boundary crossing is viewed as transgression against the entire community. Hence individuals who happen to fall in love with each other become representative of much broader, systemic forces around the maintenance of group dominance.

The stigma attached to white people married to people of color has lessened considerably since the legalization of interracial marriage in 1967; nonetheless it persists, sometimes bleeding over into stigma against the biracial children of these unions (Brackett et al. 2006). Marrying a person of color is considered non-normative behavior for a white person and is likely to engender stigma. And, while this kind of stigma certainly affects white people, this does not minimize the tremendous stigmatization and physical risk faced by the black partner in an interracial marriage or partnership; America has a long history of black men lynched for being romantically involved with white women. Both black and white women have been on the receiving end of many other forms of violence and rejection as well.

As may be seen from the examples described thus far, whiteness itself can serve as stigma in many situations where whites have physical proximity to non-whites, especially if this proximity is to blacks. The stigmatizing effect of proximity occurs almost exclusively when whites do not have direct power over the non-whites. Examples of non-stigmatizing power relationships are a white employer and a Latino/a employee, or a white coach and a black player. In such cases, whiteness assumes its normative role: dominance over non-whites. It is when the dominance of the white person is in question, and especially when the white person is subordinate to the non-white person, that whiteness as stigma might emerge.

Much attention has been paid to whites' opposition to affirmative action, which is often articulated in the terms of white victimization (Dietrich 2015). Many whites believe that they are not getting equal opportunities to jobs and college admissions; hence they regard themselves as victims of a system that systematically benefits non-whites. While this victimhood may look like stigma on the surface, the underlying phenomenon is actually quite different. The resentment of those opposed to affirmative action, some of whom may be stigmatized whites, is rooted in a perceived denial of white privilege, according to which whites are entitled to be overrepresented in professional jobs and college admission slots. This resentment underlies the formation of social movements such as the Tea Party, which are discussed in Chapter 5. Conversely, the experience of stigma is rooted in the evaluation of a white person by those whites who unambiguously have the privilege to which many whites believe they are entitled.

Defensive

In sharp contrast to the whites who experience stigma by virtue of their whiteness, another group of whites embraces its racial privilege and vociferously defends it when it is threatened. The defensive position of whites in this category can sometimes translate into an assertion of white racial privilege, even in the absence of an immediate threat. The attitudes of whites who are firmly and proudly connected to their racial identity are shaped by their expectations about what they, as a group, deserve. Their lives have largely been shaped by racial advantage, generating a sense of privilege and ownership that is difficult to dislodge and that can pose a threat to anyone who may challenge the absolute character of "white rights."

But these expectations and advantages are not often within the conscious awareness of defensive whites. These people tend rather to perceive demographic changes and changes in their relative status as a loss of community or security, and such perceptions are very much connected to racial privilege. For centuries, rights and benefits considered normal for whites have been unavailable to non-whites. This suggests that racial discrimination and animus are not necessarily triggered by flawed character or individual-level pathology but are the activation of a racial prejudice generated by structural change. The defensive reaction to loss of privilege is often evident among those who are privileged along other dimensions, such as gender and social class. For example, some whites are driven by a fear of non-whites to live in gated communities, defending whiteness and maintaining their privilege by actually walling themselves off from others (Low 2009). Defensive whites are not necessarily motivated by an absolute loss of resources; more likely, they react to a loss of the complete dominance that represented the norm for them.

One manifestation of the defensiveness shown by whites is their attempts to keep predominantly white neighborhoods racially homogenous. American history is filled with examples of whites contesting racial residential integration, both through "white flight" and through outright violence. The white privilege embraced by defensive whites demands a clear demarcation between white "turf" and non-white residential areas. Whites who experience racial change in "their" neighborhoods can be so strongly affected emotionally that they suffer something akin to trauma—an experience that is exacerbated by the fact that their adherence to the dictates of colorblindness inhibits discussion of their feelings and prevents a non-racist way of moving forward (Maly and Dalmage 2015).

A variety of institutional factors, such as racially discriminatory lending practices and racial covenants, helped create and insure racial residential segregation. In addition to these factors, whites would take collective action to keep blacks out of their neighborhoods, for example by burning crosses in blacks' yards or by firebombing blacks' homes. After discriminatory lending practices and covenants were outlawed, many whites took other steps to keep blacks out of their communities. These ranged from cold stares to protests against the construction of public housing and to outright violence. Whites in majority white neighborhoods opposed the construction of public transportation routes through their communities, as it was thought to increase the number of non-whites. In all these examples, whites are actively mobilizing their privilege to defend what they believe they own solely as a result of their whiteness.

Schools, too, were a site for the exercise of white privilege, as many whites defended majority white schools from integration with non-white students. This may have reached its apex in the public eye with the proclamation from George Wallace, governor of Alabama: "Segregation now, segregation tomorrow and segregation forever." Yet these sentiments and actions corresponding to them persisted beyond George Wallace's stand on the courthouse steps to the present time. White administrators, prodded by white citizens, drew zoning maps that maintained segregated schools. When federal desegregation orders were levied against many parts of the South, whites built private schools to remove their children from mixed-race environments. Some whites will pay a hefty premium for their houses in order to ensure that their children attend majority white schools. These decisions are often made under the guise of locating "good" schools, or schools free of the threat of violence, in order to help children to succeed. Such decisions not only lead to a division of resources between majority white and majority non-white schools, but also maintain the distance between whites and other racial groups. In addition to majority-white neighborhoods, white schools generate environments in which white children grow up with minimal exposure to people outside their race. This, in turn, contributes to a sense, among whites, of being special and of privileges attached to it. As with "their" neighborhoods, whites work to defend what they believe is theirs—the schools to which they send their children.

The defense of white privilege is evident not only in the racial preservation of white space, but also in the perception of a right to jobs and college educations. "Affirmative action"—that is, hiring and admission practices designed to increase the diversity of workplaces and schools—causes some whites to feel that their individual rights are under attack (Skrentny 1996). Selective hiring and admission practices are viewed as unfair, as whites' monopoly on employment positions and college slots is attributed to merit rather than to systematic historical advantage in securing these positions.

The circumstances of these attitudes to affirmative action are quite different from the circumstances of stigmatized whites. Rather than living on the margins of acceptability, whites who believe that they are losing out to non-whites feel that what is due to them is being stripped away from them. Mainstream—not marginal—whiteness defends perceived rights such as access to opportunities, which are implicitly biased in favor of whites. Opposition to affirmative action policies, for example, has manifested itself in a variety of ways, most notably in the political realm. Parents have complained about recruitment policies that target non-whites for admission to educational institutions, believing that their children are disadvantaged in terms of the right to access institutions such as magnet schools. And whites have infamously filed lawsuits against universities for maintaining racial preferences in admissions.

In some cases, the defensiveness that whites enact is more literal than figurative. Law enforcement has a history of disproportionately harsh treatment of non-whites—blacks in particular. Law enforcement provides a concrete, physical defense of the property and privilege of white Americans. In recent years, black Americans have actively protested law enforcement's differential treatment of whites and blacks. Blacks are more likely to be stopped through law enforcement (Warren et al. 2006) and are given longer prison sentences than whites for similar crimes (Tonry and Melewski 2008). In addition, police officers tend to use greater force when having contacts with blacks. Police often step up patrols in majority non-white neighborhoods, increasing the number of arrests among non-whites as residential segregation and racial targeting interact. In majority white public spaces—including neighborhoods—whites have reported to retail workers and to the police that blacks don't belong, and this has led to the harassment of black men and women who are simply existing in shared spaces.

Aggressive law enforcement strategies and tactics help protect white property, maintain social distance between whites and non-whites, and reduce competition for resources. Many whites are fiercely defensive of the activities of law enforcement, even when these have been demonstrably shown to result in discriminatory treatment. For example, the Black Lives Matter movement that arose in response to a number of high-profile police killings of unarmed black men was almost immediately opposed by a counter-movement called White Lives Matter. Although heralded as a push for equal treatment, the rise of this movement can be seen as reflecting the impulse of whites to defend their privileged status in America. To assert that white lives matter, or even that all lives matter, in response to a plea for equal racial treatment at the hands of police officers negates the oppression that blacks experience from an institution that has long protected the interests of whites at the expense of those of blacks.

One of the results of differential policing throughout America is the maintenance of boundaries between whites and non-whites. Such boundaries include the borders between neighborhoods, where there may be policing practices that keep under heightened surveillance the people who "don't belong" in a community (whether non-whites in a majority white neighborhood or whites in a majority non-white neighborhood). But it is not just policing that maintains neighborhood boundaries; a variety of policies and behaviors do it, thus maintaining segregation across America.

A history of discriminatory practices such as selective mortgage lending and the outright prohibition of non-whites from certain housing projects and communities generated racially segregated neighborhoods. Subsequently the boundaries between neighborhoods within these communities have often been fiercely defended by whites. Historically acts of violence and intimidation by whites against blacks who have moved into majority white neigh- borhoods have been regular occurrences. In New York City, a careful statistical analysis found that racially biased crimes against people of color were highest in majority white neighborhoods that had witnessed a recent influx of non-whites (Green et al. 1998). The key factor was not simply the racial mix of the neighborhood, or the fact that a greater number of minorities were available for whites to target; rather it was the fact that non-whites were *entering* white-dominated communities (Green et al. 1998). Whites were defending a space that they perceived as "theirs." At certain points, when violent tactics appeared not to have the desired effect, some of these whites simply decided to leave the neighborhoods—a process known as "white flight." White flight can lead to an even greater commitment to maintaining the racial boundaries around a neighborhood. Kefalas (2003) finds in her study of a white working-class neighborhood in Chicago that residents are dedicated to keeping their homes and property neat and orderly, to reflect their commitment to the community. She writes:

> For residents swept up in white flight, the experience of fleeing has made them feel victimized by the Civil Rights era and fuels their profound attachment to the area. Beltway resident and activist Lydia Donovan explains: "What you have to understand is that for many people they have had to move once or twice so what they say is based on their experience. Like when Martin Luther King marched on Chicago, he went to places like Marquette Park and so on. So, many people who live here have had to move once or twice. For them, Beltway is the last stand." (Kefalas 2003: 57–8)

A similar process explained the opposition of middle-class whites in the Canarsie neighborhood in Brooklyn, New York to the sale of homes in "their" community. Rieder (1985) finds that the white flight in nearby communities in Brooklyn led the Italian and Jewish residents of Canarsie to worry obsessively about their properties losing value if blacks were to move into "their" communities. Real estate brokers would play upon white homeowners' fear of demographic change and buy white-owned properties at a loss; this would result in a general decline in property values as a neighborhood's racial composition shifted from majority white to majority black. White residents in Canarsie were thus fervently opposed to blacks entering "their" neighborhoods and fought bitterly to prevent it. One of Rieder's respondents said: "I am not a racist. I just want to keep my community pure. I sunk every dime I have into my house and I don't want to be chased. I won't be chased" (Rieder 1985: 80).

One factor underlying whites' defense of the racial composition of the neighborhoods in which they live is the desire to maintain a white majority within schools. Since public school attendance is typically determined by residence, whites engage in white flight or seek to defend "their" neighborhoods from non-whites as a means of keeping social distance between their children and children of color. These choices are often made under the guise of school quality or safety, but *de facto* they represent a defense of the racial composition of schools. In essence, whites can have a sense of ownership over institutions that they will strive to maintain and, in some cases, bitterly defend.

Borders between whites and non-whites are not only spatial and institutional; they may also be personal. For example, some whites desire "social distance" from racial groups outside their own. According to a scale for measuring social distance developed by Emory Bogardus in the early 1920s and still in use today (Wark and Galliher 2007), forms of social distance include the willingness to interact with other groups as co-workers, neighbors, close friends, or relatives by marriage (Mather et al. 2017). The concept may also incorporate the space between different groups, in social settings such as parks, stores, or restaurants. If a group prefers to have little contact with another group in such a setting, it can be said to prefer social distance from that group. When responding to surveys such as those that will be discussed in the next chapter, many whites expressed a desire for social distance from non-whites, for example by wishing to live in neighborhoods that have substantial white populations. In addition, whites often feel some emotional distance from blacks as well. For example, 50–60 percent of the whites surveyed in the *General Social Survey* state that they feel closer to whites than to blacks (Bobo et al. 2012). Many respondents also withhold admiration and sympathy from blacks (Bobo et al. 2012). Defending majority white neighborhoods and schools represents another form of distancing behavior. Choices about maintaining all-white or majority white contacts include making decisions about where to shop, what parks to spend time in, and what tables to sit at in a restaurant.

The defense of personal space by whites has implications that extend beyond issues of racial integration.

Less social interaction between whites and non-whites results in less empathy on the part of whites. If whites hear arguments about the effects of racism on the educational and economic outcomes of blacks, Latinos/as, and American Indians, those who see these groups as abstract entities may have a more difficult time acknowledging these effects. On the other hand, many whites who have regular contact with non-whites can more readily believe in the effects of discrimination if they hear or witness accounts of it first hand. Hearing about racism from a friend or co-worker can make structural inequality personal, which can then translate into support for policies designed to ameliorate racial inequality. When whites defend their personal space from non-whites, these conversations don't happen.

Whites' ignorance about the struggles of non-whites can translate into a sense of moral superiority on their part. One common form of judgment is against non-white women (especially black women) who receive government assistance—what is called "welfare." Whites defending their position of superiority often paint a picture of welfare recipients as willingly trying to take advantage of government largesse in order to avoid work. The stereotype of the poor black woman who spends money on luxury items such as cars and jewelry is connected to the perception of black women as being fundamentally selfish and lazy. Laziness and selfishness are then compared to the opposite characteristics of whites, who are claimed to be hard-working and generous. In fact women receive increasingly stingy welfare benefits and are barely able to cover necessary expenses such as rent and food; it is not uncommon for welfare recipients to be unable to afford food by the end of the month (Edin and Lein 1997). In addition, many poor non-white women seek employment actively, in spite of an often discriminatory labor market. Whites defending their superior moral position, however, are not aware of the complexities of poor women's lives; they rely instead on stereotypes.

A related justification for whites' projections of moral superiority stems from the stereotype of the single mother, especially as applied to blacks. Black women are perceived as having numerous children despite being unable to afford their care. Just like the women who receive welfare, they are considered to be selfish—to put their own interests ahead of those of their children. Besides, some whites construe having children as a strategy for receiving money from the government: each child brings some more support. A related stereotype that is mobilized to defend the moral superiority of whites is that of the absent black father, represented as an irresponsible parent who does not care for his children. Many whites can then tell themselves that their families are superior to those of blacks, because their choices have been different.

Both the welfare recipient stereotype and the poor single mother stereotype are juxtaposed with tropes about the self-sufficiency and good judgment of whites. White claims to moral superiority vis-à-vis non-whites are a defense against questions about their own choices; and, in turn, whites' act of defending their morality, not only as individuals but also as members of their racial group, serves as protection against the judgment of others. In addition, membership in a self-proclaimed superior group is self-enhancing and a shield against claims to rights and recognition on the part of non-whites.

One of the strongest negative stereotypes that whites use to assert their own moral superiority over non-whites—especially male non-whites—is that of criminality. Fear, judgment, discrimination in hiring, and punitive public policies are some of the effects of this stereotype. In many notable incidents, this stereotype has actually led to the murder of black men, whether by police or by private citizens who made assumptions about the criminality of the victim. In other cases, black men and women have had the police called on them for the "crime" of being in a predominantly white area. Latinos/as have been thought of as criminals by virtue of simply living in the

United States. And the stereotype of American Indians as alcoholics has sometimes extended into one of American Indians as criminals.

Survey data show that many whites believe that blacks tend to commit crimes. Such data also indicate that these stereotypes influence punitive policies. The same data reveal that whites do *not* believe that whites tend to commit crimes (Peffley and Hurwitz 2002). This difference reflects an orientation toward associating whiteness with responsibility and good citizenship, while blackness represents the opposite. The perception of blacks as prone to criminal behavior determines a need to monitor and control black behavior in order to protect white values. As a result, prison sentences for crimes committed by blacks and Latinos/as tend to be longer than for crimes committed by whites (Demuth and Steffensmeier 2004). Blacks and Latinos/as are much more likely to be imprisoned than whites. When released as former felons, they are sometimes unable to vote, arguably being stripped of full citizenship. This disenfranchisement is another means of elevating the power and claims to citizenship that characterize whiteness. And the monitoring of non-whites in majority white neighborhoods helps defend the perceived safety and purity of these neighborhoods. The connection between space and crime facilitates a process whereby whites can imagine that the implications of white criminality are different from those of non-white criminality. For example, drug use by young people in white suburban areas is often viewed as an aberrant result of delinquent behavior. In non-white areas, drug use is more likely to be viewed as a pathology that requires the strict enforcement of law.

The many manifestations of defensiveness among whites—protection of white neighborhoods and schools, opposition to affirmative action, stereotyping of non-whites as criminals—are not distributed equally across whites of different social classes and ethnic identities. For example, middle-class whites are especially likely to oppose programs that set aside positions for non-white candidates in businesses, whereas working-class whites are opposed to the general idea of programs that help non-whites get ahead (Kluegel and Smith 1983). While both middle-class and working-class whites tend to prefer predominantly white neighborhoods and schools, the middle class has an ease of exit from increasingly non-white spaces that the working-class does not often have. Middle-class people can often marshal their resources to relocate to a majority white neighborhood, whereas working-class whites may not have that opportunity.

When mandatory school busing is applied to a school district, working-class whites are more likely than middle-class whites to be bused away from their neighborhoods, or to watch non-whites be moved into "their" neighborhoods. This puts working-class people in a position where they feel that they must defend their perceived right to majority white schools, while middle-class whites remain relatively unaffected. In the 1970s the struggle over school busing was brought into high relief in places like Boston, where white residents of the largely Irish American South Boston neighborhood protested against a plan to bus children from a majority black neighborhood into the community (Formisano 1991).

Ethnic identity is an important tool for whites of both middle and working classes to defend their privilege. In the current era, European ethnic identities are most likely to be claimed by older residents of urban areas (McDermott 2015). Asserting an Irish identity, for example, can lead individuals to claim that blacks and other non-white groups should receive no "special" treatment, since the Irish descendant's ancestors were discriminated against, yet managed to experience upward social mobility without the government's assistance. This account of discrimination and no assistance is problematic, as the discrimination against Irish Americans was minimal by comparison to that experienced by blacks, Latinos/as and American Indians. In addition, white ethnic groups *did* receive substantial government assistance, especially in the form of mortgage assistance and eligibility for social security assistance that comparatively few non-whites received, since occupations such as farm worker and domestic helper were prohibited from social security. These occupations were overwhelmingly held by non-whites.

All forms of white ethnic identity are problematic defenses against economic or social gains by non-whites. In some cases, ethnic identity can serve as a marker that distinguishes the individuals as something more than simply "white," although few whites feel that their ethnic identity is more important than their racial identity (Torkelson and Hartmann 2010). Colorblind understandings of whiteness that treat whites as essentially having no race have led some members of this racial group to find other identities, which will render themselves more interesting than "just" white (Waters 1990). For example, one of McKinney and Feagin's interviewees felt that being white lacked substance—that being Irish was more interesting and more important. She said: "I don't think that I have missed any opportunities or been discriminated against because I am Irish ... I think it makes good conversation" (McKinney and Feagin 2004: 85). This desire to seem distinctive in some way arguably motivates some of the interest—sometimes intense among whites—in DNA testing that can "determine" genetic racial and ethnic ancestry. By discovering that their origins lie in a particular place in the world, these whites can think about their own history and corresponding identity as something much more complex than white, as "white" is not a category used by the genetic testing services (Roth and Ivemark 2018).

Nonetheless, there was, historically, a correlation between the revival of white ethnic identification and anti-black attitudes and actions. According to Jacobson (2006: 2), "[t]he Civil Rights movement had heightened whites' consciousness of their skin privilege, rendering it not only visible but uncomfortable ... after decades of striving to conform to the Anglo-Saxon standard, descendants of earlier

European immigrants quit the melting pot. Italianness, Jewishness, Greekness and Irishness had become badges of pride, not shame." This pride was a double-edged sword. Its positive effects included renewed respect for a heritage that had once been an embarrassment. Its negative effects included justification for the assertion of white interests under the cover of a maligned minority. This was seen most notably in the opposition to school busing in Boston in the 1970s (mentioned earlier), where Irish American-identified whites organized themselves to protest against the entrance of blacks into "their" schools—as well as against having their own children bused into schools in majority black neighborhoods. The resulting conflict was thought to have solidified neighborhood boundaries and damaged black–white relations in the city for years to come. The white ethnic revival had consequences beyond Boston, however, as a combination of ethnic identity, working-class status, and clearly defined neighborhood boundaries was correlated with racial violence in multiple cities, including New York and Chicago. White ethnicity, in these cases, was a manifestation of defensive whiteness, implicated in boundary maintenance as much as embraced as a personal identity. Although white ethnic identity has significantly declined over time (Alba 1985), it is still important in localized areas in the Midwest and Northeast (such as Boston).

Transcendent

A subset of whites think about their racial identity in a way that transcends the usual bifurcation between "white" and "not white"—quite a departure from the defensive stance of many whites. This subset does not embrace whiteness wholeheartedly but identifies with one or more other racial groups. The motivations for such identifications are varied, as are the manifestations. For example, some racially progressive whites seek to abandon any active identification with whiteness while continuing to acknowledge the structural advantages that white identity has given them (Flores and Moon 2002). Other whites are attracted to the assumed cultural content of non-white identities as a means of differentiating themselves from the normative aspects of whiteness. Some may identify with a non-white racial group for material reasons (Antman and Duncan 2015). In general, attempts to transcend white identity are often criticized as lacking any awareness of the privilege whiteness bestows.

It is not unusual for multiracial young people to exhibit identity inconsistency (Kramer et al. 2015). This differs from transcendent whiteness in that such people have parents from different racial groups and elect not to identify with only one category. Research has also shown that whites who must discuss race-related topics with blacks will try to push their white identity out of their minds—to temporarily suppress their identification as white (Marshburn and Knowles 2018). Famously, in *Black like Me*, the journalist John Howard Griffin transformed his physical appearance such that he would be assumed to be black. He traveled throughout the Jim Crow South, recording the many instances of racism he encountered. His stories held great power for many white readers, who were confronted with the fact that there is nothing essential about race: exactly the same person can be treated radically differently as a result of social perceptions. While Griffin's work had considerable impact, he did not actually believe himself to be black— his identity didn't change, only others' perception of it did. By contrast, whites who seek to *transcend* whiteness have consistently thought of themselves as white, until they had a sudden break with that identity and started to consider themselves to be of a different race. Even among whites who "discover" through DNA tests that they have a multiracial heritage, only a subset will fully embrace a new *racial* identity (Roth and Ivemark 2018).

Morning (2018) describes several categories of people who claim racial group membership in ways that mark a departure from the past. The categories include "genetic members," "cosmetic members," "emotive members," and "constructed members." When these labels are applied to whites, genetic members believe that their DNA indicates that they are not "simply" white people. Other whites might have cosmetic surgery in order to take on the phenotypical characteristics of another racial group. Emotive members, such as Rachel Dolezal (a former leader of the NAACP in Spokane, Washington who was born to white parents but claimed to be black), have a strong, subjective connection to a race other than white. Constructed members are whites who feel that this racial category reflects nothing "objective, natural, or inevitable" (Morning 2018: 1066) about them; Rockquemore and Brunsma (2002) have a similar notion of transcendent race. Each of these groups of whites has in common a strong desire to be something other than simply white (or even white at all). Why would such a desire emerge?

Experiences with social class may explain some of it. Much of the American discourse about inequality concerns race—for example, whites are believed to be affluent and blacks are believed to be poor. These stereotypical associations are so strong that middle-class blacks and poor whites are often forgotten categories. Whites who have experienced difficult economic circumstances resist the racialized narrative that uses "black" and "white" as shorthand for poor and rich. Since they cannot easily shed the label "poor," some decide to shed the label "white." In this way, their class status is not a cause of stigma (as described earlier in the chapter) but becomes instead a reasonable outcome of the racial discrimination they experienced as non-whites.

One example of the connection between class status and racial transcendence is that of the Melungeons. The Melungeons are a group that claims white, black, and American Indian ancestry and has historically been

centered in Appalachia. The southern Appalachian region
has long been associated with stereotypes of poor whites
as people who live in poor housing conditions, in uncon-
ventional family formations, and in ignorance. Historically
considered an impoverished group by other residents of
Appalachia, the Melungeons have more recently been
called a "proud people" (Kennedy 1994). In recent years,
Melungeons' poverty has been attributed to a history of
racial discrimination rather than to a failure to live up
to the standards of white privilege. Paradoxically, this
shift in attribution has prompted a number of residents
in Appalachia and the nearby communities to identify as
Melungeons, despite having always considered themselves
white (and being considered as white by others).

In a study of participants at a Melungeon heritage festival
(McDermott 2010), several of those who had switched
their racial identities from white to Melungeon spoke of
being discriminated against in the past on the grounds
that they were from Appalachia. One man was refused an
apartment in Ohio because he was from eastern Kentucky,
while another woman reported being ridiculed at a business
meeting in Atlanta after the group learned that she hailed
from the Virginia mountains. People such as these, now
Melungeon-identified, experienced a combination of shame
and anger, having been treated as "white trash" from a
stigmatized region. When they discovered (or rediscovered)
the availability of the Melungeon identity through local
news stories and by word of mouth, it immediately spoke
to them. At long last they found an explanation for the
derogatory treatment they received: they had been discriminated against for being members of a *racial* group rather
than members of a social class. In the dominant discourse
about inequality in America, race is a more common and
understood marker than class. Never mind that this understanding is itself racist, since it assumes that blacks should
be poor and whites should be affluent; racial identity that is
connected to discrimination is explicable in a way that class
discrimination (especially among whites) is not.

While it is unusual for whites to shift their racial identity to black, those embracing a Melungeon identity are, in part, doing just this. In some ways this reflects the colorblind approach to racial identity described in Chapter 2, as it shares a belief that there are no significant differences between racial groups. However, Melungeons and others with transcendent white identities do actually view other races as distinctive, but they often fail to recognize the differences in lived experience between racial groups. Although identifying with black racial heritage, "Melungeon" is not coterminous with blackness, as American Indian heritage is also an important element of the identity. Native identity has become widely popular among those who, historically, have thought of themselves as white and have been thought so by others (Golbeck and Roth 2012). The explosion of interest in DNA analyses that purport to provide individual-level accounts of racial composition is partly behind this trend in identification, as is the increasing popularity of genealogical research. As with other transcendent versions of whiteness, the attachment to Native American ancestry is a way of creating distance from one's white identity while simultaneously maintaining an affiliation with its privileged status. As one of Golbeck and Roth's respondents put it,

> Well, Native Americans are in vogue now. It's all the thing to be Native American, if you can claim 'Well, I'm part Native American' because they get the passion and the glory days now of everything with the sweat lodges and medicine healing and all that, their Native spirit thing ... They may have lived as an American–Caucasian all their life and Native Americans had to go through the discrimination, and the reservation ... I guess it's kind of like an ego-status thing. (Golbeck and Roth 2012: 423–4)

This woman, who herself identifies with both her white and her American Indian heritage, senses that there is something special about being an Indian now—a specialness that whites do not have.

The number of Americans claiming American Indian identity on the US census form exploded between 1960 and 1990 (Nagel 1995). Liebler et al. (2017) find substantial variation in identifications with American Indians between 2000 and 2010. Many of those who identify themselves as American Indian on the census form do not list a tribe at all (Liebler and Zacher 2013), although tribal identity is of considerable importance to many of those with a long-standing affiliation with a tribe. These findings suggest that the Native identity is becoming increasingly popular among people who previously had had no connection with it. Some Indians have a joke about the frequency with which white Americans claim to be "part Cherokee," as this is by far the largest tribe and probably the one that most whites would be aware of. Senator Elizabeth Warren's widely reported comment about her Native American heritage earned her approbation from many quarters, as her assertion that she was part Cherokee was not strongly substantiated.

Why is there this relatively newfound desire to affiliate oneself to a group that has been highly stigmatized throughout history? A cynical response might be that individuals who would otherwise be considered white could claim to be Native American as a way of gaining affirmative action benefits. There is limited evidence for this, as affirmative action for hiring purposes may include the specification of tribal membership. In addition, many of those who claim to be American Indian are past their working years. Instead, Native American identity could serve a function that is very much related to the meaning of whiteness in America: rather than feeling part of a group that is "invisible" or "nothing," these individuals embrace the opportunity to affiliate themselves to a recognized and visible racial identity. Roth and Ivemark (2018) found that this was true for a number of the whites they interviewed about their interpretation of the results of the genealogical DNA testing they had undergone. While most of the whites who transformed their racial identities substantially after the test incorporated a Native American identity, one white southern woman incorporated a black identity, saying: "[it was not that hard] for me to find out that I was black because I don't have black skin. And not everybody knows. Maybe that's it" (2018: 175). This woman's black identity is costless: she endures none of the downsides of being black in American society, since "not everybody knows." Instead, those who find non-white identities exciting and exotic can adopt them as symbols of a richer culture and heritage than they feel their whiteness conveys, without enduring the societal cost.

Embracing non-white categories is not only about seeming more interesting, however. Since racism can be a defining feature of whiteness, there are whites who will fervently distance themselves from a group that is inherently discriminatory. Socially progressive whites can feel regret at being part of a group that has continuously oppressed people of color for centuries while at the same time gaining privileges from this oppression. Such an attitude is sometimes referred to as "white guilt." As a result of it, some of these whites seek actively to distance themselves from a polluted white identity. In contrast to poor whites, whose identity is stigmatized by virtue of their challenging the socioeconomic advantages of whiteness, progressive whites can be embarrassed by the presumed racist content of their white identities. Their shame at being white is not a result of the attitudes of others; it is caused by their own critical assessment of their group identity.

Anti-racist activists, in particular, are not at all proud of being white and see almost nothing positive about it. Hughey (2012a) argues that white anti-racists actually think about race in the same way as white nationalists—as an essentialist identity; instead they reject its oppressive power rather than champion it. Scholar-activists such as Noel Ignatiev and John Garvey (1997) encourage racially progressive whites to become "race traitors," actively confronting racism in their daily lives as a way of transcending their whiteness. They founded the journal *Race Traitor* with the tag line: "Treason to whiteness is loyalty to humanity."

People of color have a range of reactions to whites' transcendence of their racial identities, much of it critical. Among the biracial women whom Storrs (1999) interviewed and who did have some racial identity options, the attitudes to whiteness were often fraught. Rather than capitalize upon white privilege, they viewed its characteristics through the eyes of the non-white community, to whom they also belonged. As a result, a number of the interviewees went to great lengths to shed their connections with whiteness and to be considered wholly black, Asian, Mexican American, or some other non-white identity. Some wore clothing or adopted hairstyles that reflected their non-white heritage, while others would emphasize particular physical markers that were not associated with whiteness (Storrs 1999).

Of course, most non-whites do not have the option of changing their racial identity throughout the day, or even throughout their lives. Instead they are targets of discrimination as well as of stigma, regardless of what they do or think. Discovering white ancestors or rejecting their race will not change their experience of the world, as very little about their daily experiences or structural position will be different from what it was before. Since phenotype plays an outsize role in the ways in which non-whites are treated by others in interactions—for example by law enforcement officers, by store clerks, by teachers—race can be experienced as fixed rather than optional. Darker skin color has been shown to have a range of negative impacts even within racial groups. For instance, darker skinned blacks have lower educational attainment, lower incomes, and longer prison sentences than lighter skinned blacks (Hochschild 2006). Although many whites who try to transcend their whiteness are well intentioned and in some cases actively anti-racist, the experience of white privilege of those distancing themselves from their whiteness can often go unacknowledged.

The three categories of people who have a heightened awareness of their own whiteness—those for whom whiteness is visible—capture three distinct manifestations of whiteness in America. From the defensive whites who embrace their privilege and defend "their" neighborhoods from non-whites to the transcendent whites who try to distance themselves from privilege by disowning the identity, some whites have a heightened sense of their race. At the same time, each group of "whiteness visible" individuals may have little or no understanding of what the lives of non-whites are like. Awareness of whiteness does not translate into awareness of blackness, for example. Nonetheless, the situations in which whites are racially aware are as important to understand as color-blind racism, because they have implications for attitudes and actions that can shape political and social outcomes. Some of these implications will be discussed in the next chapter.

– 4 –

Attitudes and Culture

Whiteness manifests itself in various ways in American life, from the individual level to the structural. In this chapter the focus will be on the individual, micro-level expression of whites' attitudes to political and other issues. It will also be on whiteness and culture—a meso-level between individuals and institutions. Through a discussion of attitudes and culture, it is possible to discern the ways in which macro-level structural forces racialize everyday life.

White Americans consistently respond differently from non-whites to a host of questions that measure attitudes to a large variety of subjects across political, cultural, and social realms. Sometimes—especially with regard to cultural issues—white attitudes are treated simply as the generic beliefs that everyone holds. However, there is a rich tradition of studying racial differences in political attitudes. Regardless of the topic, white attitudes can provide an important window into how whiteness permeates whites' views of themselves and of the world around them. Relatedly, whites' cultural preferences in areas such as music and film open a window into the ways in which whiteness is constructed. White dominance in cultural production has also shaped how society as a whole has thought about racial difference and identity.

Why do white people think so differently from non-white people about so many things? As discussed in Chapter 2, many whites go through life in a privileged position that they never notice or examine. Non-whites are almost constantly reminded of their lack of privilege, and their thoughts and beliefs are influenced by these experiences and realizations. Whites' social and political beliefs seem like the "normal" positions to take on issues, not attitudes that are consciously shaped by experience. Consequently, whites' attitudes can be dramatically at odds with those of non-whites, whose experiences are so different.

A number of different theories have been developed to explain white racial attitudes. Several of these theories conceptualize contemporary racial attitudes as falling under the rubric of "new racism" (Krysan 2000)—forms of anti-black prejudice and opposition to race-targeted policies that are different from earlier manifestations of overt bias. "Old-fashioned racism" was once the dominant form of racial prejudice, and is still what many associate the term "racism" with today. It encompasses beliefs in the biological inferiority of blacks, the endorsement of racial discrimination in employment and education, and a strong desire for maintaining social distance (as in whites refusing to have blacks at their homes for dinner). These white supremacist ideas are still upheld by some whites today, although they are much less common than they were sixty years ago. Instead, more subtle forms of prejudice hold sway. Three of the most important of these new forms of prejudice are symbolic racism, racial resentment, and laissez-faire racism (Krysan 2000). Symbolic racism echoes the themes of colorblind racism. It encompasses four main beliefs: racial discrimination is no longer a problem, blacks don't work hard enough, black demands are unwarranted, and blacks should not receive any advantages (Tarman and Sears 2005). Like colorblindness, the dismissal of the reality of racial inequality leads whites to blame individuals for their socioeconomic status (SES) and, consequently, to oppose any policies designed to reduce inequality. Symbolic racism was developed to explain white attitudes toward policies aimed at reducing racial differences between whites and blacks, but it has been found to predict attitudes to immigration policy as well (Berg 2013).

Similarly, laissez-faire racism focuses on less overt forms of prejudice than those that were widely endorsed decades ago. As with symbolic racism, a key component of laissez-faire racism is whites' failure to support policies designed to address racial inequality. In addition, endorsing negative stereotypes of blacks and blaming blacks for their low SES are important elements in this set of attitudes (Bobo et al. 1997). Beliefs about blacks' supposed tendencies to engage in criminal behavior or to be poor are connected to whites' criticism of policies designed to reduce discrimination, as they see racial inequality as reflecting the consequences of individual behaviors.

Racial resentment is similar to other forms of modern racism, in that it focuses on whites' beliefs that blacks are granted unfair advantages (Wilson and Davis 2011). Kinder and Sanders (1996) developed a theory to explain whites' shift from thinking about blacks as biologically inferior—as "dim-witted or lazy or promiscuous" (1996: 106)—to thinking about them as not trying hard enough and using welfare when they don't really need it. Whites, in essence, are resentful of the things blacks have because they don't believe that blacks deserve them. Racial resentment reflects a "racial individualism" (Tuch and Hughes 2011) that is predicated upon white beliefs that there are not structural causes of racial inequality, but only individual ones.

The different forms of modern racism describe beliefs about race that are fairly stable. However, these attitudes are sometimes more strongly activated than others. In particular, situations in which whites feel threatened in some way—whether economically, politically, or socially—are likely to stir prejudice. These situations emerge frequently, as whites' position of dominance is often under threat. If something suggests that privilege will not be maintained, this triggers a negative response from many whites. For example, increasing numbers of non-whites moving into the country or into a majority-white neighborhood can lead whites to express increasing levels of prejudice. As the threat they perceive to their status increases, their racial animosity increases. Group threat—the fear of losing resources or status to another group—is an especially important mechanism in explaining whites' attitudes toward neighborhood racial composition. Numerical increases in the non-white population are not the only stimuli of threat. The increasing socioeconomic fortunes of a non-white group may also arouse feelings of group threat among whites. Such is the case with white attitudes toward Asian Americans in the Silicon Valley (Jiménez and Horowitz 2013); the affluent Asian American population in this part of the country engenders a sense of jealousy in whites.

As the concept of group threat implies, the context in which whites work or reside has significant implications for their political and social beliefs, as well as for their cultural preferences. The percentage of residents who are black in a city, neighborhood or metropolitan area is directly related to white racial attitudes, larger percentages of blacks being correlated with more negative attitudes held by whites vis-à-vis blacks. In addition, white racial attitudes differ between regions of the country, southern whites having a distinctive profile as especially conservative. The social class composition of an area also influences white attitudes on racial policy; whites in lower SES communities tend to have more negative racial attitudes (Oliver and Mendelberg 2000).

In addition, the degree to which whites say they are connected to their white identity in surveys correlates with their racial and political attitudes (Jardina 2019). For example, people who identify strongly as white are more likely to feel that they are losing out to non-whites (Jardina 2019). Croll (2007) finds that there is a curvi-linear relationship between a range of social and political attitudes and closeness to white identity. For example, whites with a strong racial identity were most likely to either strongly agree or strongly disagree that the United States should give everyone equal access to a good education (Croll 2007). Whites with the most and the least progressive attitudes are the most likely to be strongly connected to their racial identities, presumably because there are two distinct meanings of that connection (Croll 2007; Hughey 2012b). On the one hand, strong identifi-cation with one's white identity can reflect an awareness of white privilege, while on the other hand it can reflect a pride in one's race.

Most of our knowledge about white attitudes comes from survey data. Several major US surveys, such as the General Social Survey and the American National Election Study, have been regularly administered for decades. Since they use random samples of the US population, the attitudes they capture can be thought to be representative of the nation as a whole. From surveys such as these, social scientists have found that, in general, whites hold distinctive attitudes. The major attitudinal trends will be reviewed in the rest of the chapter.

Social Attitudes

Whites' social attitudes are in some ways distinct from those of other groups, although there are several key issues about which there is little disagreement between whites and non-whites. General attitudes toward gays and lesbians, for example, have been found to be roughly the same among blacks and whites (Jenkins et al. 2009).

Attitudes regarding criminal justice are another matter. Whites are substantially more punitive than blacks, being much more likely than blacks to favor the death penalty

(Bobo and Johnson 2004). Whites' punitive stances extend to juveniles, and support for treating young people like adults in the court system is even more likely to come from whites, who have more racial resentment—which suggests that juvenile delinquency has been "racialized" over time (Pickett and Chiricos 2012). In other words, black children have been judged relatively more harshly over time simply because of their race.

Abortion is another contentious social issue that displays different patterns of support along the racial spectrum. Support for legalized abortion—a consistently polarizing issue in American life—is greater among blacks than among whites. However, whites were more supportive than blacks in the early 1970s (Strickler and Danigelis 2002). This trend is driven in part by increasing support for abortion among black females (Carter et al. 2009). Regarding the environment, too, non-whites hold different attitudes from those of whites. Perceptions of environmental risk, including concerns about climate change, are greater among non-whites than among whites (Macias 2016).

Attitudes toward Politics

Whites differ from other racial groups in their political attitudes across almost every dimension. They are more likely than non-white groups to identify as conservative and as Republican. Preferences for various government programs and opinions as to their desirability also differ by race. For example, blacks are more likely than whites to support social welfare programs. Trust in the government, on the other hand, tends to be greater among whites— unless the political leader is black (Howell and Fagan 1988).

Several studies have found that between whites and non-whites there are differences not only in their respective political attitudes, but also in their beliefs about whites themselves—and substantial differences at that. For instance, Jardina (2019) finds that white identity, and especially "white consciousness," predict a host of political and racial attitudes. White consciousness is defined as whites' sense of connection to whites as a group—a sense of belonging as well as shared political interests. White consciousness was an especially robust predictor of support for candidates in the 2016 presidential election, where it predicted support for Donald Trump and opposition to Bernie Sanders, Ted Cruz, and Marco Rubio. The opposition to Republicans like Cruz and Rubio suggests that white-conscious individuals are concerned more about the candidate's race than about his or her political platforms. Schildkraut (2017) finds the same relationship between preferences for white candidates and both white identity and whites' sense of linked fate—linked, that is, with the fate of other whites.

Attitudes toward Race and Immigration

Whites have more negative attitudes toward immigration and toward policies designed to ameliorate racial inequality than do non-whites; this is especially true of working-class whites (e.g. Gest 2016). Whites are also more likely than non-whites to endorse negative racial stereotypes and to make a host of other negative judgments about other racial groups. Among the working class, these judgments are perhaps a way of dealing with a sense of their own marginality (Moss 2003), or with feeling directly threatened by non-whites in terms of status or resources. Two of the most consistently reliable predictors of attitudes toward race and immigration are education and political beliefs: those with college degrees are more positive toward non-whites and more supportive of immigration. Self-identified political conservatives are most likely to harbor negative racial attitudes and to favor restrictive immigration policies.

There has been a dramatic shift in the kinds of racial attitudes that whites have held over time. During the Jim Crow era, many whites were adamantly opposed to inter-racial contact in many forms, including through interracial marriage, residential integration, and school integration. Significant numbers believed in the biological inferiority of blacks. Over time, the endorsement of these beliefs gradually waned, and they were replaced by subtler forms of resentment and opposition to racial policies (Bobo et al. 2012), which some argue are driven by feelings of anger (Banks and Valentino 2012). Whites still endorse negative racial stereotypes, but these are likely to follow a gradient and to be less categorical than in previous years (Bobo et al. 2012).

The role of economic threat in shaping white attitudes is complicated. Those who express concerns about their personal economic situation are, for example, inclined to believe that lack of motivation is a factor in explaining blacks' relative lack of success (Miller 2016). However, economic threat has not been consistently linked to beliefs about immigration. Threat, as measured by the proportion of non-whites in whites' cities and neighborhoods, *has* been linked to a range of racial beliefs and attitudes, such as stereotypes about Latinos/as' work ethic and anti-Asian stereotypes (Samson and Bobo 2014). In general, larger proportions of non-whites in a community are correlated with greater prejudice.

Other forms of threat can also influence white attitudes toward non-whites. Whites are concerned with defending their privileged status, whether it be measured in dollars or in esteem. Challenges to the dominant position or status of whites in the social hierarchy can trigger a sense of threat and a corresponding increase in negative attitudes toward non-whites. For example, Samson (2013) finds that white college students at elite schools feel threatened by Asian American students, as they worry that their status as the most meritorious will be challenged by the superior academic performance of many Asian Americans.

When white survey respondents are told that there is a large percentage of Asian Americans at the University of California, they think that less weight should be placed on grade point averages (GPAs) as a criterion for college admission; when they are told that the percentage is small, they think otherwise. When white survey respondents are told that there is a larger percentage of black Americans, GPA is given great importance as a criterion for admission. Whites who perceive that they have been discriminated against are more likely to feel threatened by non-whites (McDermott et al. 2019).

Beliefs about affirmative action are influenced not only by a sense of threat but also by colorblind ideology (Knowles et al. 2014). When whites deny that they have any privilege and distance themselves from their white identity, their support for affirmative action drops (Knowles et al. 2014). Opposition to affirmative action is also found, perhaps unsurprisingly, among whites who actually think that whites are being discriminated *against* (Knowles et al. 2014).

The forms of racial identity adopted by whites also influence racial attitudes. In the United States, those who have a strong sense of white racial identity are much more likely to feel threatened by immigration and to believe that it has "negative consequences for the nation" (Jardina 2019: 185). Interestingly, Jardina (2019) finds that opposition to immigration from people who identify as white increases as whites are informed about demographic change. This strongly suggests that whites' negative attitudes toward immigration are fueled by a sense of group threat. The difference between whites who embrace diversity and whites who do not is not predicted, however, simply by the strength of their connections to being white, but also by the meaning that whiteness has for them (Goren and Plaut 2012). For example, whites who recognize the power inherent in whiteness are most supportive of diversity, those who take pride in being white are the least supportive, and those who are only weakly attached to their white identity stake out a neutral position (Goren and Plaut 2012). A feeling of closeness to whites is an even more powerful predictor of anti-black prejudice than are interracial interactions among a sample of elite white college students (Byrd 2014).

Whiteness and Culture

Culture has diverse meanings. While it includes various forms of intellectual production, such as film, literature and music, it can also refer to a set of patterned practices and beliefs that comprise the lives of individuals. Baldwin et al. (2005) provide dozens of definitions of culture, ranging from language and symbols to political ideology. Culture is a "seamless" part of our lives, and "we all live in part by way of habits, manners, recipes, rules, mores, ethics, rituals, procedures, and other cognitive or symbolic devices" (Battani et al. 2003: 9–10). Culture can be produced at the level of a group—for example, there has long been debate, in sociology and public policy, about a "culture of poverty." According to early versions of theories around this concept, those who live below the poverty line hold beliefs and engage in practices that ensure the continuation of their impoverished status across generations. Although many of these early theories have been largely debunked, there is nonetheless sustained interest in the cultural aspects of poverty (Small et al. 2010) and social class in general. In this sense, classes are defined not merely by objective criteria, such as how much education or income people have, but also by how people behave and the values they have.

Historically, cultures of different racial groups have not been considered in the same way as cultures of different classes. Just as in racial identity, where whiteness is treated as the default norm, in cultural life, too, "culture" is often limited to the dominant racial group in society. Thus cultural practices associated with non-white groups are typically referred to with modifiers such as "black culture" or "Latino culture." By contrast, "white culture" is a rarely used concept. Whiteness is intertwined with culture in the way it is discussed, both in popular discourse and by scholars (though to a lesser extent). The fact that whiteness is seen to be the default mode of acting and knowing about the world is sometimes referred to as "white normativity" (Ward 2008). Organizational cultures can reflect whiteness, even though culture as an institution ostensibly has nothing to do with race. For example, emphasis on a high degree of individualism expresses priorities that are embedded in the white cultural outlook, in contrast to the more collectivist practices of other racial groups. Ward (2008) finds that white culture was dominant in an LGBT organization that was designed to reduce structural inequality, not contribute to it. For example, the adoption of corporatist practices that included holding a "diversity day" made non-whites feel as if the organization were culturally white. Most of the non-whites in the organization had dealt with issues related to diversity on a daily basis for much of their lives; a special day celebrating diversity seemed implicitly designed for whites.

Many of the taken-for-granted components of culture have their roots in white-dominated practices. In some cases, this is a result of the explicit exclusion of non-whites from participating. In other cases, racial segregation produced a pattern of differential diffusion of practices. For example, foods that emerged from Scandinavian settlers in the Midwest developed in a context where very few non-whites were present, and thus became artifacts of whiteness. Foods that developed in the southern United States (outside Appalachia), where contacts between whites and blacks were frequent, did not produce such distinctively "white" foods.

Occasionally cultural objects—such as art, music, or television—and cultural practices are defined by pundits and scholars as being rooted in whiteness. This process of defining objects as "white" has ranged from the serious to the tongue in cheek. Multiple calls challenging the white-dominated canon in literature as required reading for all students have resulted in a racial (and gender) diversification of the works of fiction that are taught in many college classes. On a lighter note, the book entitled *Stuff White People Like* and the successful blog attached to it (http://stuffwhitepeoplelike.com) itemize the practices and preferences associated with whiteness, such as camping and reading the Sunday *New York Times*. Such stereotypes of behaviors and practices may seem light-hearted, but they belie the reality of whiteness' domination of so much of what has grown to be called "American."

Many musical genres have come to be associated with particular racial groups. Country music, for example, is sometimes thought to be a "white" musical genre. The majority of performers, listeners, and producers are white, and the lyrics and style are also associated with whiteness (Mann 2008). "The whiteness to which it calls is ... not class-specific, it is unapologetically American and Christian, defiantly average, realistic, and tired of political correctness and elitism" (Mann 2012: 87). Mann (2008) makes the argument that country music not only reflects whiteness but also produces it. The nostalgia inherent in the lyrics creates attachment to a seemingly grander, white-dominated past, which attracts white listeners while it also bolsters white identity. Non-white country music performers such as Charley Pride are often referred to with a racial descriptor such as "black country singer," as if to be distinguished from ordinary country singers (Mann 2008). This reflects the stereotype of country music as music by and for whites only.

Classical music has also historically been associated with whiteness. Although Asians and Asian Americans make up a non-negligible proportion of performers and consumers (Yang 2007), the history of much classical music is rooted in Western European traditions. About twice as many whites attend classical music concerts or say they like classical music as do blacks (DiMaggio and

Ostrower 1990). In 2014, Latino/a musicians made up only 2.5 percent of orchestras and blacks only 1.8 percent (League of American Orchestras 2016). About 4 percent of conductors were black, while approximately 8 percent were Latino/a (League of American Orchestras 2016). Hence classical music's association with whiteness is well deserved.

Whites who perform music associated with non-white groups, for example hip-hop, which is associated with blackness, can face criticism either for being cultural imperialists or for attempting to abandon their whiteness. While some might argue that all music belongs to all groups in an uncomplicated fashion, "by borrowing the experiences of people of color embedded in their art, young whites can have a sense of culture without questioning their whiteness" (McKinney and Feagin 2004). Some whites participating in hip-hop music perform and consume that music in such a way that it is less connected to race: they effectively deracialize it (Rodriquez 2006). When cultural authenticity is strongly connected to race, whites would not have claim to that authenticity. If, on the other hand, authenticity is more loosely connected to race, or connected to a more fluid sense of identity, then a malleable form of whiteness may be enacted by performers and consumers of music with roots in the black community.

Film also has a strong association with whiteness; the notion of "white movies" seems almost absurd, as so much of the film industry has been white-dominated throughout its history. One genre of film that is especially relevant to the study of white culture is that of the "white savior film." In these movies, a leading white character heroically saves a grateful non-white follower or dependant from a grim fate. Feagin (2013) describes several of these films, for example *The Blind Side*, in which a southern upper middle-class white woman rescues a black teenager from a life of poverty, or *Dances with Wolves*, in which a white soldier leads Native Americans away from peril.

A related genre is the "white messiah" film. In this common style of movie, a white male hero emerges as the leader of a rejected group to save a population of oppressed, often dark-skinned followers (Vera and Gordon 2003). Although the white messiah sometimes operates alone or in the interest of the nation or world as a whole, he often acts so as to lead or save a grateful non-white population. Much like the white savior film, the white messiah film is self-serving for whites and condescending toward non-whites. It "enable(s) the white self to live with itself and to absolve [itself of] the guilt of racism by portraying the white as noble and self-sacrificing on behalf of other races" (Vera and Gordon 2003: 116). These messages are uncritically accepted by viewing audiences when no alternative narrative is provided.

In sum, white racial identity encompasses a wide range of attitudes and is associated with different cultural practices. Whiteness shapes how individuals think about the world, even though the role of race in their own thoughts and preferences may be opaque to them. Political attitudes and social beliefs shape how we move through the world, and the kind of music we listen to shapes our understanding of the world. When whites think and behave differently from non-whites, this results in racial differentiation, which furthers the distance between groups and can contribute to racial inequality. While few would wish that everyone be the same, an awareness of the connection between what we like and believe and our racial identity could bridge some of the racial differences in America. However, as will be seen in the next chapter, organized forms of whiteness can forge these connections in ways that exacerbate racial differences.

– 5 –

Whiteness Mobilized

Just as whiteness is intertwined throughout a number of American institutions, so too is it intimately connected to organized social movements. This connection between white racial identity and social movements seems obvious when it comes to white supremacist movements, since the primary goal of many such organizations is to further the interests of the white race. Examples include the Ku Klux Klan and neo-Nazis. For such activists, whiteness is hardly the invisible identity it is for many whites; rather it is central to their way of being in the world (Blee 2002). They view whites as something akin to a nation: an "imagined community" that may some day recognize its own interests and act on them (Blee 2002). Perhaps surprisingly, given some of their rhetoric about the general superiority of the white race, some white supremacists actually define whiteness by the criterion of *loyalty* to "the white race," without making any appeal to biological factors; thus anti-racist whites would not count as truly white, for example (Blee 2002).

Whiteness is also *indirectly* involved in other movements and campaigns, not only in the racial makeup of the membership but also in the centrality of the interests of white Americans, which comes down, specifically, to the goals of the movement. Goals of this sort would be advocacy for a limited government or for a change in the tax structure that directly benefits whites over other racial groups—goals held by groups such as the Tea Party; or advocacy for reduced immigration, which maintains whites' numerical majority in the United States—a goal of the Minuteman Project. A number of these groups disavow, on the surface, any racial preferences or targeting, arguing instead that their positions or activities benefit everyone equally. It is vital for any social movement to maintain a positive public image; this is a more difficult task if an organization is believed to be racialist (Schroer 2008). Yet, even without any overt claim to a pro-white agenda, there are clear racial disparities, both in membership composition and in the movements' strategies, which are implicitly organized around whiteness.

Whiteness is salient not only to white supremacist movements but also to movements organized by white anti-racist activists. In the latter, white members overtly recognize their racial privilege and argue for its abolition. Hence white racial identity is central to their activities. Hughey (2012b) finds that the understanding of white identity is actually quite similar in racists and in anti-racists: both have an essentialist understanding of what it means to be white. This mirrors Jardina's (2019) finding that white identity is most important to Americans who place themselves furthest to the left and furthest to the right politically.

Whiteness is intertwined throughout a number of social movements in America, be they rooted in the overt expression of white identity or based on the implicit furtherance of positions and policies that support whites as a group. These movements are integral to the foundation upon which white dominance—together with challenges to it—rests. Members of such movements typically find their commitments to the superiority of whiteness strengthened (Blee and Yates 2015). Such organizations are capable not only of bringing about change in race relations—and even in government policy (e.g. a revision of the tax code)—but also of laying bare the ways in which whiteness is understood and functions in everyday life.

Explicit Use of Whiteness in Social Movements

Most of the social movement organizations that *explicitly* advocate for whites and promote their interests are white supremacist or racialist movements. The term "white supremacist" encompasses a motley group of activists whose organizations range from historically prominent ones, such as the Ku Klux Klan, to small, recently formed movements. The number of such groups is growing. The Southern Poverty Law Center estimated that there were 1,020 hate groups in the United States in 2018; this number went up from 892 in 2015 (Beirich 2019). Hate crimes, sometimes committed by such groups, are also on the rise. There were 5,790 hate crimes in 2012; just five years later, that number had climbed to 7,106 (Federal Bureau of Investigation 2018).

White supremacist movements have a long and ugly history in the United States. The Ku Klux Klan, for example, was formed in 1865 in Pulaski, Tennessee, initially as a small organization whose goal was more to startle than to intimidate (Chalmers 1987). It quickly grew into a violent organization that used the cover of disguise by night to murder and maim blacks throughout the South. During its resurgence during the 1920s, it became especially powerful, drawing hundreds of thousands to an event in Indiana, for example (McVeigh 2009). By mid-century up to 5 million white men belonged to the Klan, preparing for a race war that pitted white Protestants against everyone else—and especially Jews, blacks, and Catholics during the earlier years of the organization (MacLean 1995).

But the Klan is not only an organization of the past. In recent years, like many white supremacist organizations, it has taken to online forums to build community and further its agenda (Bostdorff 2004). In addition to reiterating its racist and anti-Semitic views, it also issues calls for violence. For embedded in the message of white racial uplift is an animosity toward non-whites, especially blacks, which is so powerful that it often prescribes violence. The use of the Internet makes messages of violence much easier to communicate.

The Klan's violent deployment of white racial superiority is rooted in its members' belief that whiteness equals humanity and blackness does not. In this way, the exercise of violence is not seen as a troubling act, as it might otherwise. To members of the Klan, there is a clear, physical definition of race that is connected to superior traits. For example, in reply to the question "What does it mean to be white?," one of Dentice and Bugg's (2016: 112) Klansmen respondents states the following: "Highly identifiable DNA of the people of Europe/Eurasia (considered by some anthropologists to have evolved from both Cro-Magnon and Neanderthal)." Others talk of the greatness of European civilizations. In addition, they feel that their need for social distance from those whom they do not regard as fully human is justified (and this need for social distance continues to be evinced in some of the attitudinal data discussed in Chapter 4). Whiteness is thus thought to be not only morally superior but also physically and materially righteous, in a way in which other races are not. During its period of rapid growth during the 1920s, the Klan managed to deemphasize its commitment to violence and to emphasize its religious and charitable impulses as a means of appearing more "palatable" to outsiders, but the underlying ideology persisted nonetheless (Alexander 2015).

Many rules and rituals support the Klan's ideology. Perhaps best known are the flowing robes and pointed white hats that are worn during ceremonies, and the rides during which blacks are intimidated and worse. Equally infamous are the cross burnings, in which giant wooden crosses are burned in front of the homes of blacks as a warning against behaviors disliked by the Klan, such as blacks' movement into predominantly white neighborhoods. However, the largest cross burnings were held in open fields, solely for the members themselves, who stood in awe of the spectacle. Rallies and parades have been another prominent feature of Klan activities—although, as Wade (1998: viii) notes, "today ... there are more bystanders hooting and jeering at them than there are Klansmen themselves."

Although this rich history looms largely in the past, the Klan is not merely an historical artifact. Today it has only a fraction of the membership it had in its heyday during the 1920s; nonetheless it continues to be implicated in attempts at racial violence. As recently as 2018, for instance, Brandon LeCroy of Greenwood, South Carolina tried to hire a member of the Klan to lynch his black neighbor and leave a burning cross in his yard (The State 2019). The FBI broke up the plot and LeCroy was sentenced to ten years in prison. Nonetheless, the fact that he not only thought he was able to contact a member of the organization but was also familiar with its tropes and its penchant for racist violence is testament to the Klan's continuing relevance.

Neo-Nazis also have a lengthy history in the United States (although shorter than the Klan's). Perhaps most strongly associated with the vehement anti-Semitism propagated by Adolf Hitler and his regime, neo-Nazis also put forward a virulent strain of general white supremacism. They consider race to be biologically rooted and associate "white" with intelligence, virility, physical prowess, and a host of other positive characteristics. Like other white supremacist groups, they do not view non-white groups as being fully human (or not quite as fully as whites). This makes it easy for them to reconcile morally with violence, segregation, and other dehumanizing attacks.

Neo-Nazis, including racists skinheads, have attracted a number of young people—(including women—and have been especially active online (Blee 2002; Burris et al. 2000). Ideologically, they are very much obsessed with Jews as the enemy and draw the boundaries of whiteness around religion as well as around race. But they also consider blacks, Latinos/as, and Asians to be "mud people" controlled by Jews, and therefore deserving to be treated as enemies (Ezekiel 2002). Neo-Nazis assert the superiority of whiteness at every turn, in both discursive and violent ways.

The neo-Nazi movement was thrust into the spotlight in the summer of 2017, when the avowed Nazi James Fields drove his car into a crowd of counter-protesters at a white supremacist rally in Charlottesville, Virginia, killing one and injuring thirty-three others. He was sentenced to life in prison. His actions were the manifestation of his commitment to the ideals of "the racial purity doctrine of the Third Reich" (*Washington Post*, 12/11/18), and they exposed a national audience to the impact of an ideology of extreme white superiority. Explicit displays of white power and supremacy do not stop at postings in Internet chat rooms or marches through town; they also demand the eradication of those who exist outside the groups' defined boundaries of whiteness.

The neo-Nazi Richard Spencer is credited with being a founder of the alt-right (Hawley 2017). "Alt-right" is a relatively recent description, which encompasses a loosely organized set of activists and their followers, many of them linked through a sometimes anonymous presence in online forums. They agitate for extremist positions that often have a pro-white slant. An online presence had long been important to white supremacist groups; one of the most popular forums, Stormfront, was founded in 1996. Sites such as these provide white supremacists with an online community that makes it easy for them to recruit others who share their beliefs in the superiority of whiteness (Daniels 2009). Although some of the members and leaders of the alt-right disavow white supremacy and claim nationalist positions instead, their ideology nonetheless shares tenets with white nationalism (Hawley 2017). Called "the banner of white identity politics" by Richard Spencer (as quoted in Hawley 2017: 68), the alt-right has surged in popularity and mainstream representation since the election of Donald Trump and his appointment of alt-right stalwart Steve Bannon to his cabinet.

Although less committed to a program of active violence than the Ku Klux Klan or neo-Nazis, neo-Confederate groups are also clear about the importance of maintaining social distance between whites and other groups. This often explicit concern with whiteness—sometimes cloaked as involvement with heritage—sets them apart from groups that are careful to avoid any mentions of race or association with those who make such mentions. "Neo-Confederates … propose that cultures and ethno-racial characteristics are inherited, that behaviors are innate and immutable, and that it is unnatural and thus impossible for two or more ethno-racial groups to co-exist in the same space on equal terms" (Hague and Sebesta 2009). Consequently neo-Confederates are bitterly opposed to any government programs designed to increase racial integration or reduce inequality, including affirmative action or equal spending for schools. This opposition reflects an ideology that is common to all white supremacist organizations—namely the belief that whites are victims (Berbrier 2000). A component of the assertive whiteness put forward by neo-Confederates and similar groups is that no group should ever have resources greater than their own. This extends to emotional and psychological resources such as self-esteem, in addition to material resources such as advantages in securing employment (Berbrier 2000).

Ultimately neo-Confederates want a return to the Jim Crow South. This belief is related to an overarching assumption that the Civil War was not fought over slavery, but that the South had every right to secede because states' rights were not being honored. These groups will distinguish their position on race from that of other white supremacist groups, often disclaiming racism altogether. Instead, they direct their animus at the federal government, which intervened to secure civil rights for black Americans (Hague and Sebesta 2009). Neo-Confederates argue clearly and overtly for whites' legal and social dominance, which was once total and complete, yet they feel compelled, on occasion, to disguise their position by adopting the language of opposition to governmental intervention. This tactic is especially common among those whose embrace of white interests is even more implicit, for example Tea Party activists (Blee and Yates 2015). Neo-Confederates' desire for racial segregation renders their overt deployment of white racial identity much more visible than it is in many other movements.

According to the Southern Poverty Law Center, neo-Confederate groups have shifted closer to other white supremacist groups in recent years. In 2017, several members of the League of the South were charged in the beating of a black man in a parking garage; another was arrested for involvement in an assault in Charlottesville. Although violence has not been as fundamental to the ideology of the neo-Confederates as it has been to neo-Nazis, it is a natural outgrowth of a commitment to the fundamental biological superiority of the white race that dehumanizes all those outside its boundaries.

The Council of Conservative Citizens (CCC) is another white supremacist group that has evolved from older groups committed to Jim Crow laws and rigid racial separation. White Citizens Councils are relics of the mid-twentieth-century South that battled against the end of segregation. In 1985, the CCC obtained the White Citizens Councils' mailing lists; since then it has developed into an objectively white supremacist group, according to the Southern Poverty Law Center. Its own statement of principles is this: "We ... oppose all efforts to mix the races of mankind, to promote non-white races over the European-American people through so-called 'affirmative action' and similar measures, to destroy or denigrate the European–American heritage, including the heritage of the Southern people, and to force the integration of the races" (http://conservative-headlines.org/statement-of-principles). The organization's website posts a list of crimes committed by blacks against whites.

It was one of these lists of blacks' offenses against white people on a CCC website that inspired Dylann Roof—the white supremacist murderer of nine black parishioners in Charleston, South Carolina—to begin enacting his racist philosophy. Word of the role that the CCC played in this notorious hate crime gave the organization considerable notoriety, although the CCC sought to distance itself from the act. It wanted instead to claim a more mainstream identity, while at the same time emphasizing the superiority of whiteness. Supporting this mainstream identity, several nationally prominent politicians such as Mike Huckabee, Trent Lott, and Haley Barbour spoke at CCC events (https://www.nytimes.com/2015/06/23/us/politics/views-on-race-and-gop-ties-define-group-council-of-conservative-citizens.html). Members of the CCC injected themselves into protests, defending the flying of the confederate flag over the state capital of South Carolina even as they rejoiced in the fact that the National Association for the Advancement of Colored People (NAACP) boycotted the state on the grounds that it flew the flag. Although the CCC itself does not deploy a violent posse at night, as did the Ku Klux Klan, and does not purposely target individuals for murder, as do the neo-Nazis, it nonetheless uses words recklessly, to incite others to violence. At the root of its philosophy is an adherence to the fundamental, biological superiority of whiteness.

Counter-intuitively, social movements that, politically, couldn't be further apart from the CCC also have platforms that construct white racial identity in essentialist ways. Some anti-racist activist organizations believe that race is a fundamental, immutable characteristic that carries privilege. However, they believe that this privilege is morally corrupt and undeserved rather than a God-given right that should be upheld. Their belief in race as fundamental to the essence of a person translates into a commitment to eradicating all the benefits attached to the race into which they are born—or a commitment to becoming "less white" (Hughey 2012b: 2). Not all anti-racist activists fit this mold; some think of racial identity as a more constructed and mutable category, with whiteness taking different forms over time and space. However, groups such as the Whites for Racial Justice (WRJ), which Hughey (2012b) studies, recommend ways of transcending a fixed category rather than of adapting or rethinking a mutable one.

Hughey (2010) argues that WRJ members share a sense of whiteness as a distinct "groupness," which constitutes the basis for action. They set boundaries between their own white racial group and other races, and they do so in a variety of ways. While anti-racist organizations might ordinarily be associated with progressive ideas about whites (e.g. that they are always victimizers and never victims; and this is indeed what the literature of WRJ suggests), Hughey finds instead that WJR members understand whites to be stigmatized in much the same way as white supremacist groups do. For example, one respondent complained that "white identity is 'in the line of fire ... I can't say what I feel about racism, even though I am critiquing it!'" (Hughey 2010: 1296). There is a surprising sense of being under attack, even as the group wishes to discard its unearned privileges. At the same time, WRJ places a premium on "conscious whiteness," that is, on beliefs that fit with the outlook of the group rather than with mainstream notions of white identity. Whites who do not follow these seemingly rational, simplistic notions of racial identity and privilege are marginalized (Hughey 2010). In this way the anti-racist organization reifies white identity and is constantly patrolling its boundaries.

Implicit Use of Whiteness in Social Movements

It is easy to see the role of whiteness in movements such as the Ku Klux Klan or neo-Nazis, whose overt statements about the superiority of the white (or "Aryan") race are foundational to the group's mission. It is more difficult to discern the ways in which whiteness is embedded in social movements that do not mention race directly in their platforms or recruitment materials—a process similar to the invisible whiteness described in Chapter 2. It is just as important to consider the ways in which such organizations mobilize racial identity in the service of goals that further the interests of whites in America as it is to understand other types of organizations. One might argue that all movements have to do with whiteness to a certain extent, given the degree to which race is intertwined with every institution in society. Yet some organizations have goals that involve the interests of whites more directly than do others.

One of these organizations is the Tea Party. Emerging in 2009, in the wake of Barack Obama's election to the presidency, the Tea Party began as a group of largely Republican adherents who fervently opposed the Affordable Care and Patient Protection Act (Obamacare). While they failed in their attempts to derail the legislation, they were successful in their efforts to help the Republican Party take back the majority of seats in the US House of Representatives in 2010 (Skocpol and Williamson 2016). Tea Party activists are in favor of small government, low taxes, and major cuts to social programs. They also strongly support restrictions on immigration and "subscribe to harsh generalizations about immigration and blacks" (Skocpol and Williamson 2016: 11). However, unlike in the movements discussed earlier, Skocpol and Williamson find that "there is little evidence that most individual Tea Partiers reject normal interactions with people of other races" and that leaders make an effort to include blacks in organizational events.

Yet at the same time, at a Tea Party rally on Freedom Plaza in Washington, DC in 2010, Zernike (2010) saw signs that read "Barack Hussein Obama, go back to Kenya"—a racist message designed to suggest that the nation's first black president was not actually an American citizen but an African. Zernike also observed, however, pleas among organizers that Tea Party members reach out to people of color in their community, so as to include them as potential members. Why is there such a disconnect between the overtly racist words and images of anti-black and anti-immigrant statements and attacks on the president, on the one hand, and, on the other, an apparently strongly felt desire not to let race determine the methods, goals, or membership of the movement?

The platform of the Tea Party, which is anchored in the commitment to small government and low taxes, represents the interests of white America, even without any explicit intention to do so. Since a number of social programs are means-tested (especially those attacked by the Tea Party), they are more likely to benefit those with low incomes. Since non-whites are more likely to have low incomes than whites, whites are more likely to benefit from the eradication of these programs and the reallocation of the money elsewhere. Since whites have higher average incomes than non-whites, they are more likely to pay higher taxes than non-whites (in absolute dollars). As a result, lowering taxes is more likely to benefit whites than non-whites. Hence the Tea Party is a social movement that is very much about furthering the interests of white America, albeit without claiming to do so. Although its leadership emphasizes the importance of recruiting from multiple racial backgrounds, its membership is 91 percent white (Maxwell and Parent 2012).

Another loose agglomeration of organizations that implicitly appeals to whiteness by virtue of its membership and goals is the militia movement. "Militia" is a term applied to tightly organized groups that were part of the patriot movement of the 1990s. It also designates loose bands that prepare for a final showdown with the US government; they do so through weekend guerilla warfare training sessions and through the purchase of survivalist products (Kimmel and Ferber 2009). Unlike the Tea Party, militias advocate violence for the achievement of their goals, and this culminated most notably in the bombing of the federal building in Oklahoma City in 1995. The goals themselves often involve separation from, if not strong opposition to, the US government. While some of these groups dovetail with white supremacist organizations—especially the rural movements of the 1990s (Kimmel and Ferber 2009)—others make official statements to the effect that their ideologies are race-neutral. Nonetheless, just like the Tea Party and other, less vociferously anti-government organizations, militias oppose fiercely any social programs from the government, and this resistance carries an implicit declaration that the privilege of whiteness is inherent and justified.

A related group of volunteers who proclaim themselves defenders of America are the members of the Minuteman Project. Again, this group does not claim to have racial superiority as a central element of its platform, yet its primary goal is to prevent undocumented migrants from entering the United States from across the Mexican border. Given the racial composition of the migrants the Minutemen seek to apprehend, their actions reflect a belief in white ownership of the right to inhabit space. The Minutemen Civilian Defense Corps was founded in 2005 by a former kindergarten teacher and its purpose was to patrol the Mexico–US border in search of undocumented immigrants. The group claimed that its first patrol led to the arrest of 335 undocumented immigrants (Yoxall 2006). As we have seen in the Tea Party, leaders claimed that the Minutemen Corps was open to members of all races; they also encouraged non-whites to participate. Their colorblindness—described in Chapter 2—takes the familiar form of belief in the sameness of all racial groups, accompanied by denial that their goals and behaviors privilege whiteness. Although the Minutemen describe themselves as welcoming to all races, almost all participants are white (Yoxall 2006). Perhaps more troubling is the fact that white supremacists have been drawn to the group's overall denigration of undocumented immigrants in ways that often shade into anti-Mexican racism (Yoxall 2006).

Progressive social movements may also be implicitly influenced by whiteness. Such is the case with the inter-racial movement Center for a Fair Economy (CFE) studied by Beeman (2015). CFE is a grassroots organization that fights for policies that benefit working-class people, non-whites, immigrants, and other communities affected by social inequality. Unlike most of the other groups discussed in this chapter, CFE is populated by both white and non-white activists. One white activist that Beeman interviewed is strongly committed to racial justice and recognizes the role that white privilege has played in her own life, yet she resolutely avoids discussions of racism with others in the group. Her concern is that "talking about that stuff ... can take a huge nosedive" (Beeman 2015: 128), meaning that relationships between whites and non-whites in the movement could quickly become fraught if any discussion of racism is to be attempted. As a result, the daily activities of a movement that is in part based on a commitment to racial justice implicitly support a tenet of colorblindness—not talking about racism.

Organized Whiteness

Whiteness can be conceptualized in many different ways: as part of the structural fabric of the country (or world), as an identity, as the basis of culture, or as a property of institutions. While all these dimensions highlight the great force of whiteness to shape every aspect of life in America, whiteness gains a particular kind of power when considered as a basic element in the organization of social movements. Perhaps the chief reason for this is the direct mobilization of whiteness as a vehicle of violence. Throughout the history of the United States, social movements organized around maintaining the superiority of the white race have advocated and used violence as a means of subjugating non-white populations (Blee 2005). While the state has engaged in the violent enforcement of white privilege, movement organizations have expanded the areas from which recruits could be drawn and have made white supremacist ideologies explicit. Organizations that place the assertion of the superiority of the white race at the center exhibit the visible whiteness described in Chapter 3, as their members not only are conscious of racial difference but also embrace it with pride.

Memberships of white supremacist organizations have fluctuated in number over time. But, regardless of their actual size and strength, the symbolic power of these organizations has been profound. Their uniforms—the white hoods of the Ku Klux Klan, the shaved heads of racist skinheads—are designed to intimidate. The primary goal of white supremacist organizations such as these is to enforce white dominance through any means necessary, including violence. Anything can be good reason for a violent response, no matter whether it results in injury or death. Underlying this ideology is an assumption that whiteness equals human and non-whiteness equals sub-human. White supremacy is the most extreme manifestation of whiteness as privilege and represents the uncomfortable and ugly corollary of the belief that some lives are more valuable than others.

The social movements discussed in this chapter that have advocated violence are relatively stable and long-lived, with the exception of some of the militias. There are also large numbers of sporadically formed and short-lived movements, often organized around a single issue such as the maintenance of neighborhood boundaries, that advocate and sometimes practice violence. All share an ability to enforce whiteness as the principal organizing force in American society. Regardless of how much other whites in society support (maybe tacitly) or abhor the tactics of these groups, their ideologies and behaviors have played an important part in securing white dominance, which in turn has maintained white privilege throughout America.

Fortunately this bleak reality is not the only one involving whiteness and social movements. I noted in Chapter 4 that people who are strongly attached to their white identities need not be white supremacists; they can be aware of their white privilege and actually be racially progressive. As we have seen with the white social justice group that Matthew Hughey studied, there are groups that mobilize their white racial identity with the intention of making it serve the goal of reducing white racial privilege. Throughout history, very many other groups have deployed whiteness so as to bring about change in the direction of racial equality rather than shoring up white dominance. Many of these movements have embraced non-violence; but not all have. Perhaps most historically notable is the group led by abolitionist John Brown, who led a raid on an army depot in Harper's Ferry, West Virginia in 1859. Furious with the institution of slavery, Brown was prepared to lead a revolt of slaves with the munitions he stole at Harper's Ferry. But his plan failed and he was executed. Although Brown's commitment to eradicating what had been in many ways the ultimate embodiment of white privilege—slavery—involved violence, many white abolitionists thought that the dictates of their own whiteness required tireless commitment to ending the practice. Hence the connection between whiteness and organized movements for change need not be one rooted in dominance and oppression; it can also be a story of seeking positive social change.

Perhaps the most complicated ways in which whiteness manifests itself in social movements are those in which a platform that represents white interests and an overwhelmingly white membership are paired with an official statement of group goals that eschews any formal commitment to whiteness. Groups with an implicit connection to white interests have been numerous throughout the social and political landscape of American history—from violently anti-government organizations such as the militias to the more politically mainstream, non-violent Tea Party. The overwhelmingly white members of these groups would typically not think of themselves as belonging to a group organized around its own racial interests; yet this is arguably the situation, whether they think it or not. It is not, however, only anti-government groups or groups in favor of small government that put forward an implicitly white agenda. Movements that organize around keeping low-income housing outside the perceived boundaries of a neighborhood similarly act in the interest of maintaining racially segregated communities; they act to protect their privilege as whites. Such organizations may work explicitly with criteria that are not racially exclusive; in consequence members would not see themselves as pursuing racial interests. Yet this is in substance what they do.

Ultimately, whiteness as manifested in social movements has the same powerful effects as in other institutions, cultural practices, and interactions. It serves to reinscribe dominant social relations and to give access to resources. Its effects are sometimes obvious, sometimes subtle. One way in which these social movements are set apart from many other institutions is that, in the vast majority of cases, whites enlist in them voluntarily—their white identities are actively mobilized rather than passively acted upon. For this reason alone, the social movement organizations are worthy of special consideration.

− 6 −

The Future of White Racial Identity

The future of white racial identity in the United States is tied to the shrinking size of the white population. Since 1790, when the census began keeping count of the racial composition of the US population, the proportion of whites had been fairly stable—until the past several decades. In 1790, 81 percent of the country's population was white; 90 percent was white in 1940, when this segment peaked in the United States. In the 2010 census, only 69 percent of the population consisted of non-Hispanic whites (Hispanic whites are whites who claim both white race and Hispanic or Latino ethnicity). Demographers predict that only a minority of the country's population will be white by the mid-century—44 percent in 2060, which would represent a 9 percent drop in the size of the white population from 2016 (Vespa et al. 2018). Whites are the only racial or ethnic group anticipated to shrink as a proportion of the US population. As mentioned in Chapter 1, they are already a minority among 15-year-olds and under (Frey 2019).

Although the possibility of a "majority-minority country" made headlines when demographers first made such pronouncements, in reality many regions of the United

States have long had minority white populations. Hawaii, for example, has never been a majority white state, and New Mexico has been majority Hispanic since the early 1990s. In the late nineteenth century, both Louisiana and South Carolina were minority white states. Yet the country as a whole has always been majority white, and much of the country's imagery—expressed in figures such as Uncle Sam—has often presented itself as such. Many states in New England have been over 95 percent white throughout their entire history. It is in this context that the notion of an impending majority non-white America resonates so forcefully.

The Effects of a Shrinking White Population

The overall decline in the proportion of the white American population is a phenomenon unlikely to pass unnoticed. Each announcement of its impending shift to a majority-minority group by government agencies, demographers, or journalists generates a new spate of either hand-wringing or rejoicing in different contingents of the population. As a structural phenomenon and as a form of identity that undergirds interactions and attitudes, whiteness is not only a function of the size of the white population. White institutional dominance does not depend on how many whites are present in institutions like schools or corporations, but is a product of the goals of organizations. If they are designed so as to maintain the current distribution of wealth and educational advantages, then the size of the white population will not matter, as resources will still be divided unequally by race. White privilege is unlikely to change simply because the size of the white population decreases; there are many colonial and postcolonial societies that provide examples of the domination of a small white population over a large non-white one. Apartheid-era South Africa is one notorious example. Nonetheless, shifting numbers do reflect shifting patterns of political strength, of social contact, and of symbolic representation that have real implications for the meaning of whiteness in American society. Much as whites living in majority non-white neighborhoods become conscious of their whiteness, as described in Chapter 3, this consciousness could emerge at a national level. However, the ways in which these changing demographics will shape what whiteness means and how it is experienced are not at all clear.

The immediate response from some white commentators and other white individuals was to express alarm at the radical changes that the declining numerical significance of the white population would bring about. They voiced worries that the fundamental character of the United States might change, and concerns about the degree to which whites might be represented in politics and other institutions. As one might expect, these preoccupations were especially prominent among those on the far right, who were also concerned that rates of immigration were too high.

Conversely, others were thrilled that whites would no longer be a majority. Many of those who were excited by this possibility were members of non-white groups (none of which would be in the majority in a majority-minority America) who saw a possibility for increased opportunity if white dominance waned. However, a number of whites were also cheered by the demographic shift, as supporters of the Democratic Party believed that their party's chances of victory improved as the proportion of whites in the electorate declined. Others also welcomed the opportunity to experience greater racial and ethnic diversity in their lives.

Hence whites have two quite different responses to changing racial demographics. One is a sense of threat; the other is a sense of excitement. What distinguishes these two responses, and the groups of whites aligned with them, from each other? In general, threat is experienced by those who feel that they have something to lose if a change occurs in the current state of affairs. There are many whites who believe that they have something to lose materially if the numbers of their racial group decline; there are many, too, who believe that they will lose the status attached to their group if their numbers decline. Finally, there are whites who are threatened by a sense of the unfamiliar. When life in a country that has been represented and understood as a "white" nation is subject to change, whites may wonder about their place in the new social order.

On the other hand, whites who look forward to a shrinking white population view whiteness as problematic, or as connected to values and a history that they find objectionable. As they feel that white numerical dominance is lessening, they may hope that the practices and beliefs correlated with it also lessen to the same extent. The chief expression of this positive reaction to demographic change among some whites is the belief that the political change ushered in by a declining white population will benefit the parties and causes they support. Since non-whites are disproportionately likely to hold liberal political positions, white liberals are encouraged to see a greater proportion of non-whites in the population.

Although the population of whites who are cheered by demographic change is not negligible, the whites who feel threatened by, or at least concerned about, the impending majority-minority populations have made themselves known as a numerically greater presence. Fear of losing status and resources is a powerful motivator and can lead to negative attitudes as well as to extreme actions. The threat experienced by rapid change has direct implications for white people's experience and understanding of their racial identity. In the near future, white Americans are likely to respond to their shrinking numbers in one of two ways. One strategy would be to strengthen the boundaries around whiteness: whites would be careful to demarcate who is "really" white, maintaining a sense of racial purity that should defend their identity in the face of an influx of people who might seem like foreign threats to their culture and ways of life. The other strategy would be the polar opposite. Rather than seeking to maintain any sort of racial purity, whites threatened by a reduction in their numerical dominance might instead seek to *weaken* the boundaries around whiteness. Far from upholding a rigid adherence to some particular ancestral pedigree or phenotype, they would consider bestowing full white status to groups of "honorary whites" such as light-skinned Latinos/as or some Asian groups (Bonilla-Silva 2004), thus preserving a white majority.

Stronger Boundaries around Whiteness

The idea of strengthening the boundaries around white racial identity at a time of decline in the number of whites may seem strange. Why wouldn't whites want to *increase* their numbers through a more expansive definition of whiteness, not help them go down even further? Yet such restrictions make sense if one considers the feelings of threat that underlie many whites' reactions to demographic change in the first place. When numerical dominance is equated with cultural dominance, for example, the loss of cultural dominance would mean that non-white groups might come to have more influence throughout a range of media and other representations that had once been largely controlled by whites. If the boundaries around "white" culture were to be hardened, then the significance and, perhaps, the corresponding dominance of whiteness might be reinforced in the face of change.

The boundaries around whiteness may ultimately be drawn by any person or group. However, it is one of the privileges of whiteness that it has "the power to name and shape identities ... [it] has the ability to limit access to those resources to those who reflect its own image" (Flagg 2005: 6). Hence the strengthening and weakening of boundaries around whiteness will always be an interactive process, yet one ultimately policed by the dominant group. Whites will be those defending the border, just as they have been since the origins of whiteness in America in the seventeenth century.

Some observers see the increasing focus on the US–Mexico border as a reflection of this contestation of the boundary between whiteness and brownness. As the demographic shifts resulting in a smaller white population in the United States are driven largely by immigration, it is logical to expect threatened whites to focus their attention upon the nearest border with a majority non-white country. The border then serves symbolic purposes, such as forging "whiteness as Americanness" (Bebout 2016: 202). It also serves as a literal line in the sand—a line drawn to keep non-whiteness out of America.

The sharpening of racial boundaries is not only a matter of maintaining cultural dominance, however. As greater numbers of non-white immigrants enter the United States and interracial marriage rates continue to go up, the multiracial population of the country quickly grows. Multiracial Americans self-identify across a range of categories, depending on factors such as physical appearance, education, gender, and the racial composition of the neighborhood (Davenport 2016; Herman 2004; Rockquemore and Brunsma 2002). Non-multiracials who currently identify as white accept multiracials as "white" to varying degrees, and the same is true of demographers, who count them. There are those who are clear that "multiracial" is a distinct category, which should not be considered white under any circumstance, while others hold on to something akin to the old "one-drop rule," which states that even one drop of non-white (originally black) blood renders a person non-white. "White" should be reserved, in their minds, only for those who are of European ancestry.

The one-drop rule reflects a long-standing practice in the United States of defining whiteness by what it is not rather than by what it is (Byrd 2017). Strengthening the boundaries around whiteness would not necessarily involve a more rigid and restrictive definition of whiteness itself, but could instead imply more expansive and rigidly enforced categories of non-whiteness. These would encompass not only multiracials but also groups such as people from the Middle East and light-skinned Latinos/as. If such groups were rigidly defined as not-white in official classifications as well as in daily social life, then the boundaries around whiteness would grow stronger without the meaning of whiteness changing at all.

Weaker Boundaries around Whiteness

During the late nineteenth and early twentieth century, the classification of Irish people (Ignatiev 1995), Italians, and other Southern and Eastern Europeans (Barrett and Roediger 1997) and Jews (Brodkin 1998; Jacobson 1999) as white was more tenuous than it is today. There was discrimination against European ethnic groups in hiring practices, and even mainstream publications used racist imagery to portray these groups. Italians were linked with Africans, and Greeks were subject to anti-black slurs (Barrett and Roediger 1997). There is little controversy as to the whiteness of these groups today. Whites who identify with their ethnic origins actually have a *stronger* connection with whiteness than do non-ethnic whites (Torkelson and Hartmann 2019). While anti-Semitism is still an all-too-present factor in American life—especially among far-right groups—there is in effect no anti-ethnic sentiment against European ethnic groups and they are rarely racialized other than as whites. One might point to these changes as examples of the malleability of whiteness. Groups that were thought to fall outside its boundaries one century ago are unquestionably within it today; hence it is plausible that groups we consider non-white today would come to be thought of as white a century from now. For whites who are concerned about demographic change, the potential for the increasing size of the white population might bring some relief. For many others—members of all racial groups—who give demographic change little thought, such shifting boundaries around whiteness are a likely reality, given the patterns of racial identity and change throughout American history.

The sociologists Herbert Gans (2012) and Eduardo Bonilla-Silva (2004) have written about some possible futures in case the current boundary around whiteness shifts and new groups come to be considered white. Both authors point to the importance of social class in determining who is accepted into the socially dominant "white" group, ethnic groups that are primarily poor and working class being the least likely to penetrate the white boundary. Gans and Bonilla-Silva also note that blacks are likely to anchor the lowest status rung in America's racial hierarchy, much as they have since the advent of slavery. This is illustrated by the comments that a white female respondent from an historically white working-class neighborhood made to Warren and Twine (1997: 212): "Blacks are not allowed to move into this area, but Mexicans and Asians are different—they can blend." The boundary between whiteness and blackness is rigid and profound.

Gans strongly believes that a white minority is not coming into existence anytime soon, that the "whitening" process has already begun. Although he notes that trends in immigration as well as in racial classification are difficult to predict, the steadily rising rate of interracial marriages seems destined to increase the numbers of people considered to be white. The process of whitening is not a simple one; it depends on factors such as the size of the non-white group and the social class of its members. A small middle-class group is likely to whiten much more rapidly than a large working-class group. And, of course, those who are less segregated from whites residentially and occupationally are likely to whiten more quickly than people isolated in enclaves (Gans 2012). Ultimately,

Gans believes that the United States is currently organized around a tripartite racial hierarchy in which those at the top include not only people formally considered white, but also "[w]hitenened Asians, Latinos and some others" (Gans 2012: 272). Implicit in Gans's whitening thesis is the notion of "ethnoracial diversity" (Jiménez et al. 2015), according to which racial groups are not to be considered uniform entities. Ethnoracial diversity is especially likely to occur when immigration status varies in significant ways within racial groups. For example, native-born whites are much more likely to be prejudiced against Latino/a immigrants than against any other group, but less likely to be prejudiced against Asian immigrants than against others, including whites (Jiménez et al. 2015). These findings suggest that the whitening process may be quicker for Asian immigrants than for others and that blacks may be shut out from it entirely.

Bonilla-Silva draws conclusions similar to those of Gans about the future of whiteness in America, contrasting changes among those in the dominant category (primarily whites) with little movement among those who currently occupy the most oppressed position on the spectrum (such as blacks). The triracial system that Bonilla-Silva envisions reflects an expansion of the boundaries of whiteness that takes place at least partly in response to increasing numbers of non-whites: the dominant white population strives to maintain its power by changing the criteria but not the meaning of the racial category of white. In other words, people may no longer need to show direct European descent on both parental sides in order to be considered white; they may be Indian, Asian, or Latino/a on one side. Nonetheless, whiteness would still be conferred only upon people who are phenotypically white, share the cultural preferences of the dominant racial group and class in America, and do not challenge in any way the privileged nature and superiority of what it means to be white. Hence the criteria necessary to attain whiteness might change, but the meaning of whiteness would not.

Bonilla-Silva's triracial system comprises three categories. The first, that of whites, includes people who are currently thought of as white as well as "assimilated" Latinos/as and Native Americans. Assimilated, in this sense, means incorporated into white American life—its attitudes, culture, neighborhoods, norms; hence whites readily treat a person in this category as "one of us." The second group is that of honorary whites. This neither-white-nor-black group includes most Asian Americans, light-skinned Latinos/as, and Middle Eastern Americans. Finally, the collective black category is made up of those currently categorized as black, as well as of Native Americans living on reservations, dark-skinned Latinos/as, and some of the lowest income Asian American groups. Multiracial groups are alternately categorized as whites or honorary whites, which reflects the fluid nature of these racial boundaries. Categorization as honorary white, as opposed to collective black, is an approximation of how threatening a group seems to the dominant white group (for a complete list of Bonilla-Silva's racial group categorizations, see Bonilla-Silva 2004: 933).

As every racial group is an arbitrary social construction, the rationale for drawing boundary lines between groups is generally rooted in the factors that maintain the privilege, status and power that the categories emerged to protect. In the case of whiteness in twenty-first-century America, the threat to this protection comes from a group's power to challenge the status quo. Groups that have the least to gain from the current political, social, and economic arrangements thus pose the greatest threat; they are therefore the least likely to be considered white when boundaries shift. Blacks challenging police shootings, Latino/a immigrants struggling to find jobs, and American Indians protesting against the building of a pipeline on their reservation provide lasting images of threat to whites, images that set those groups apart as decidedly "not-white." Conversely, one can imagine groups that are currently not considered white but are wholly invested in conforming to the rules and rituals of white-dominated society. The trajectory of their racial classification over time might look very different.

Is There an Ideal Form of Whiteness?

Much of what has been discussed in this book paints an unflattering portrait of whiteness. Whether considered as a hegemonic feature of every institution in our lives, as a descriptor of the fundamental character of the structure of our country's laws and economy, or as a generic name for the ways in which self-identified whites think about the meanings that this identity holds for them, whiteness is always implicated in the oppression against non-whites on which its own power and privilege rest. This raises a question. Is there a way in which whiteness can be mobilized as a force for justice rather than as a force opposed to it?

Several scholars and activists have attempted to answer this question. One of the defining features of whiteness has long been its invisibility. White people in the United States have neither noticed nor cared about being white because they did not have to: their taken-for-granted status as dominant actors in society has made self-awareness unnecessary, even superfluous. Tropp and Barlow (2018) find that whites need not maintain this pose of ignorance about racial inequality. When whites have the kind of contact with non-whites that causes them to be psychologically invested in what happens to members of these groups, their blindness to the existence of white privilege fades. This suggests that reducing segregation—especially social segregation—might be a means of shifting the ways in which whiteness currently shapes the perspectives of white Americans.

Reducing social segregation is part of the purpose of multicultural education initiatives such as intergroup dialogues, which seek to upend white college students' tacit connection to their privilege by encouraging critical dialogues with members of other racial groups. There are numerous critiques of such programs; for example, it is objected that they place on non-white students the burden of educating white students (although intra-group dialogues aim to alleviate this problem), or that their impact is uncertain in the long term. However, particularly engaged instructors can make a difference, as they encourage whites to think critically about their own racial identity (Cabrera 2012). When students learn how to recognize their privilege and engage in anti-racist efforts, they can influence members of their broader communities to become concerned about racial inequality (Ford and Orlandella 2015). While a push toward developing friendships and engaging in honest dialogue can only help improve interracial interactions, ultimately it may be the sheer number of interactions that improves race relations (Richeson and Shelton 2007). Even though negative interactions can activate a negative form of white identity, whites are better able to observe their own racial identity as something visible rather than hidden. If whites move beyond noticing their whiteness and recognizing its connection to privilege to actively engaging with non-whites and institutions, the nature of whiteness itself may begin to change.

Alternatively, whites could oscillate between periods of considering whiteness as just one of many multicultural identities and periods of defensively maintaining white privilege (Doane 1997b). Doane notes that the future may bring increased racial conflict and strife, with whites doubling down on their privilege. On the other hand, more vociferous calls for racial justice could mitigate whites' attachment to such privileges. Frankenburg (1993) finds, in her interviews with white women, that there are three primary discourses around race that these women use, somewhat interchangeably, and that the frequency of use varies across women. First, essentialist racism hearkens back to earliest forms of thinking about race—as a property that resides in the physicality of the person. This discourse was less often used than the second: color- or power-evasiveness, which is very similar to colorblind racism in that it deflects claims about whites' explicit role in perpetuating racial inequality. But the third type of discourse that Frankenburg found reflects a more critical and engaged perspective on whiteness: that of "race-cognizant reassertions." This perspective demonstrates awareness of structural inequality and a championing of marginalized groups (Frankenburg 1993). Ultimately, however, whiteness will never simply become a cultural identity or be reflected in a critical discourse; it will always be fundamentally connected to privilege (Doane 1997b).

In 2018, Robin DiAngelo's *White Fragility* garnered considerable attention. It outlined the defensive ways in which whites responded to black accusations of racism. D'Angelo used her analysis of the reasons for these defensive reactions to suggest how whites could engage in building "authentic cross-racial relationships" (DiAngelo 2018: 148). An important part of such relationships is for whites to acknowledge when they have engaged in racist actions—even (or perhaps especially) when there was no racist intention—and to repair the damage that has been done. Denial and silence are the antithesis of healthy inter-racial relationships. For DiAngelo, this involves being *less* white—a distancing from white identity. To the extent that one acts in solidarity with the dominant orientations of whites—"white silence and white solidarity ... privileging the comfort of white people over the pain of racism for people of color" (2018: 150)—one is working against racial justice. There is no possibility of a positive white identity.

One way of thinking about whiteness in a more positive light in the future is to consider it a condition of privi-leged awareness. Whiteness is inextricably, permanently bound up with privilege. The institutions that the country is built upon and that have transmitted wealth and oppor-tunity for generations have benefitted whites and ensured their status as the normatively dominant racial group. To do anything but acknowledge this reality would be to deny the very meaning of whiteness. Nonetheless, simply acknowledging this reality (or, worse, embracing it) merely reproduces the system of racial injustice. The task is to turn people's awareness of this privilege into a commitment to transforming the structures that brought it into being. Words such as "transformation" suggest lofty actions, for example revolution or acts of resistance; but this need not be the case at all. Besides, it would not be possible for a white person to reject every benefit of white privilege in his or her life. Rather, what is needed is a constant awareness of the ways in which privilege is conferred and maintained in American society. Such awareness can generate a way of life in which whites are able to act with respect for other racial groups and to put their own accomplishments into perspective. In short, it would give them an angle on their own privilege that gets much closer to that of non-white groups.

In many ways, whiteness has been fundamental to the creation and evolution of America. The country was built on slavery, whose premise was the dehumanization of people who were not white. Since that period in the past, the boundary between those who are able to fully enjoy the privileges of property, wealth, and political participation has been drawn around whiteness. Many lives have been lost and other lives have been foreshortened because of the magical line drawn between white and not-white. While the line is sometimes neat and straight, this is not always so. Poor white southerners may die of malnutrition as they cling to white supremacist ideologies, while white affluent college students may give their lives for racial justice. White identity manifests itself in a great variety of ways, ranging from the defensive and potentially violent to the transcendent and potentially naïve. Whiteness is structure, identity, culture, institutions, and individual acts that accumulate day after day, across centuries. Whiteness plays a major role in US politics (Jardina 2019), where the defense of white privilege and white concerns about the "threat" posed by non-whites shape the government and the contours of campaigns. Ultimately, without understanding the way whiteness operates in America, one cannot fully understand the country itself.

References

Alba, Richard D. 1985. "The Twilight of Ethnicity among Americans of European Ancestry: The Case of Italians." *Ethnic and Racial Studies* 8(1): 134–58.

Alba, Richard D. 2016. "The Likely Persistence of a White Majority: How Census Bureau Statistics Have Misled Thinking about the American Future." *American Prospect* (Winter): 67–71.

Alcoff, Linda Martín. 2015. *The Future of Whiteness*. Cambridge: Polity.

Alexander, Charles C. 2015. *The Ku Klux Klan in the Southwest*. Lexington: University Press of Kentucky.

Antman, Francisca and Brian Duncan. 2015. "Incentives to Identify: Racial Identity in the Age of Affirmative Action." *Review of Economics and Statistics* 97(3): 710–13.

Arena, John. 2003. "Race and Hegemony: The Neoliberal Transformation of the Black Urban Regime and Working-Class Resistance." *American Behavioral Scientist* 47(3): 352–80.

Artz, Lee and Bren Ortega Murphy. 2000. *Cultural Hegemony in the United States*. Thousand Oaks, CA: SAGE.

Baldwin, John R., Sandra L. Faulkner, Michael L. Hecht, and Sheryl L. Lindsley. 2005. *Redefining Culture: Perspectives Across the Disciplines*. Mahwah, NJ: Routledge.

Banks, Antoine J. and Nicholas A. Valentino. 2012. "Emotional

Substrates of White Racial Attitudes." *American Journal of Political Science* 56(2): 286–97.

Barreto, Manuela. 2015. "Experiencing and Coping with Social Stigma." In *APA Handbook of Personality and Social Psychology*, vol. 2: *Group Processes*, edited by M. Mikulincer and P. R. Shaver, pp. 473–506. Washington, DC: American Psychological Association.

Barrett, James E. and David Roediger. 1997. "How White People Became White." In *Critical White Studies: Looking Behind the Mirror*, edited by R. Delgado and J. Stefancic, pp. 402–6. Philadelphia, PA: Temple University Press.

Barthe, Emmanuel P., Matthew Charles Leone, and B. Grant Stitt. 2014. "Trailer Parks as Hotbeds of Crime: Fact or Fiction?" *Issues in Social Science* 2(2). doi: 10.5296/iss.v2i2.6402.

Battani, Marshall, John R. Hall, and Mary Jo Neitz. 2003. *Sociology on Culture*. London: Routledge.

Bebout, Lee. 2016. *Whiteness on the Border: Mapping the US Racial Imagination in Brown and White*. New York: NYU Press.

Beeman, Angie. 2015. "Walk the Walk but Don't Talk the Talk: The Strategic Use of Color-Blind Ideology in an Interracial Social Movement Organization." *Sociological Forum* 30: 127–47.

Beirich, Heidi. 2019. "Rage against Change: White Supremacy Flourishes amid Fears of Immigration and Nation's Shifting Demographics." *Intelligence Report* 166: 35–42.

Bell, Jeannine. 2013. *Hate Thy Neighbor: Move-in Violence and the Persistence of Racial Segregation in American Housing*. New York: NYU Press.

Berbrier, Mitch. 2000. "The Victim Ideology of White Supremacists and White Separatists in the United States." *Sociological Focus* 33(2): 175–91.

Berg, Justin Allen. 2013. "Opposition to Pro-Immigrant Public Policy: Symbolic Racism and Group Threat." *Sociological Inquiry* 83(1): 1–31.

Bettie, Julie. 2014. *Women without Class: Girls, Race, and Identity*. Berkeley: University of California Press.

Blee, Kathleen M. 2002. *Inside Organized Racism: Women in the Hate Movement*. Berkeley: University of California Press.

Blee, Kathleen M. 2005. "Racial Violence in the United States." *Ethnic and Racial Studies* 28(4): 599–619.

Blee, Kathleen M. and Elizabeth A. Yates. 2015. "The Place of Race in Conservative and Far-Right Movements." *Sociology of Race and Ethnicity* 1(1): 127–36.

Bobo, Lawrence D., Camille Z. Charles, Maria Krysan, Alicia D. Simmons, and George M. Fredrickson. 2012. "The Real Record on Racial Attitudes." In *Social Trends in American Life: Findings from the General Social Survey since 1972*, edited by Peter Marsden, pp. 47–86. Princeton, NJ: Princeton University Press.

Bobo, Lawrence D. and Devon Johnson. 2004. "A Taste for Punishment: Black and White Americans' Views on the Death Penalty and the War on Drugs." *Du Bois Review: Social Science Research on Race* 1(1): 151–80.

Bobo, Lawrence D., James R. Kluegel, and Ryan A. Smith. 1997. "Laissez-Faire Racism: The Crystallization of a Kinder, Gentler, Antiblack Ideology." In *Racial Attitudes in the 1990s: Continuity and Change*, edited by S. A. Tuch and J. K. Martin, pp. 93–120. Greenwood, CT: Praeger.

Bonilla-Silva, Eduardo. 2004. "From Bi-Racial to Tri-Racial: Towards a New System of Racial Stratification in the USA." *Ethnic and Racial Studies* 27(6): 931–50.

Bonilla-Silva, Eduardo. 2012. "The Invisible Weight of Whiteness: The Racial Grammar of Everyday Life in Contemporary America." *Ethnic and Racial Studies* 35(2): 173–94.

Bonilla-Silva, Eduardo. 2013. *Racism without Racists: Color-Blind Racism and the Persistence of Racial Inequality in America*. Lanham, MD: Rowman & Littlefield.

Bostdorff, Denise M. 2004. "The Internet Rhetoric of the Ku Klux Klan: A Case Study in Web Site Community Building Run Amok." *Communication Studies* 55(2): 340–61.

Brackett, Kimberly P., Ann Marcus, Nelya J. McKenzie, Larry C. Mullins, Zongli Tang, and Annette M. Allen. 2006. "The Effects of Multiracial Identification on Students' Perceptions of Racism." *Social Science Journal* 43(3): 437–44.

Brodkin, Karen. 1998. *How Jews Became White Folks and What That Says about Race in America*. New Brunswick, NJ: Rutgers University Press.

Brooks, Richard R. W. and Carol M. Rose. 2013. *Saving the Neighborhood: Racially Restrictive Covenants, Law, and Social Norms*. Cambridge, MA: Harvard University Press.

Brown, Tony N. 2008. "Race, Racism, and Mental Health:

Elaboration of Critical Race Theory's Contribution to the Sociology of Mental Health." *Contemporary Justice Review* 11(1): 53–62.

Bucholz, Emily M., Ma Shuangge, Sharon-Lise T. Normand, and Harlan M. Krumholz. 2015. "Race, Socioeconomic Status, and Life Expectancy after Acute Myocardial Infarction." *Circulation* 132(14): 1338–46.

Burke, Meghan A. 2016. "New Frontiers in the Study of Color-Blind Racism: A Materialist Approach." *Social Currents* 3(2): 103–9.

Burke, Meghan A. 2019. *Colorblind Racism*. Cambridge: Polity.

Burris, Val, Emery Smith, and Ann Strahm. 2000. "White Supremacist Networks on the Internet." *Sociological Focus* 33(2): 215–35.

Byrd, William Carson. 2014. "Cross-Racial Interactions during College: A Longitudinal Study of Four Forms of Interracial Interactions among Elite White College Students." *Societies* 4(2): 265–95.

Byrd, William Carson. 2017. "Inflective and Reflective Whiteness in the Sociology of Race and Ethnicity: A Comment on an Integrative Framework for the Field." *Ethnic and Racial Studies* 40(13): 2226–31.

Cabrera, Nolan L. 2012. "Working through Whiteness: White, Male College Students Challenging Racism." *Review of Higher Education* 35(3): 375–401.

Callais, Todd M. 2010. "Controversial Mascots: Authority and Racial Hegemony in the Maintenance of Deviant Symbols." *Sociological Focus* 43(1): 61–81.

Carter, J. Scott, Shannon Carter, and Jamie Dodge. 2009. "Trends in Abortion Attitudes by Race and Gender: A Reassessment over a Four-Decade Period." *Journal of Sociological Research* 1(1): 1–17.

Case, Anne and Angus Deaton. 2015. "Rising Morbidity and Mortality in Midlife among White Non-Hispanic Americans in the 21st Century." *Proceedings of the National Academy of Sciences of the United States of America* 112(49): 15078–83.

Chalmers, David Mark. 1987. *Hooded Americanism: The History of the Ku Klux Klan*. Durham, NC: Duke University Press.

Collins, Patricia Hill. 2015. "Intersectionality's Definitional Dilemmas." *Annual Review of Sociology* 41(1): 1–20.

Craig, Maureen A. and Jennifer A. Richeson. 2014a. "More Diverse Yet Less Tolerant? How the Increasingly Diverse Racial Landscape Affects White Americans' Racial Attitudes." *Personality and Social Psychology Bulletin* 40(6): 750–61.

Craig, Maureen A. and Jennifer A. Richeson. 2014b. "On the Precipice of a 'Majority–Minority' America: Perceived Status Threat from the Racial Demographic Shift Affects White Americans' Political Ideology." *Psychological Science* 25(6): 1189–97.

Crenshaw, Kimberlé. 1989. "Demarginalizing the Intersection of Race and Sex: A Black Feminist Critique of Antidiscrimination Doctrine, Feminist Theory and Antiracist Politics." *University of Chicago Legal Forum* 1989(1). doi: 10.1007/978-94-007-6730-0_1-1.

Croll, Paul R. 2007. "Modeling Determinants of White Racial Identity: Results from a New National Survey." *Social Forces* 86(2): 613–42.

Daniels, Jessie. 2009. *Cyber Racism: White Supremacy Online and the New Attack on Civil Rights*. Lanham, MD: Rowman & Littlefield.

Davenport, Lauren D. 2016. "The Role of Gender, Class, and Religion in Biracial Americans' Racial Labeling Decisions." *American Sociological Review* 81(1): 57–84.

Demuth, Stephen and Darrell Steffensmeier. 2004. "Ethnicity Effects on Sentence Outcomes in Large Urban Courts: Comparisons Among White, Black, and Hispanic Defendants." *Social Science Quarterly* 85(4): 994–1011.

Dentice, Dianne and David Bugg. 2016. "Fighting for the Right to Be White: A Case Study in White Racial Identity." *Journal of Hate Studies* 12(1): 101–28.

DiAngelo, Robin J. 2018. *White Fragility: Why It's So Hard for White People to Talk about Racism*. Boston, MA: Beacon Press.

Dietrich, David R. 2015. "Racially Charged Cookies and White Scholarships: Anti-Affirmative Action Protests on American College Campuses." *Sociological Focus* 48(2): 105–25.

DiMaggio, Paul and Francie Ostrower. 1990. "Participation in the Arts by Black and White Americans." *Social Forces* 68(3): 753–78.

Doane, Ashley W. 1997a. "Dominant Group Ethnic Identity

in the United States: The Role of 'Hidden' Ethnicity in Intergroup Relations." *Sociological Quarterly* 38(3): 375–97.

Doane, Ashley W. 1997b. "White Identity and Race Relations in the 1990s." In *Perspectives on Current Social Problems*, edited by G. L. Carter, pp. 151–9. Boston, MA: Allyn & Bacon.

Doane, Ashley W. and Eduardo Bonilla-Silva, eds. 2003. *White Out: The Continuing Significance of Racism*. New York: Routledge.

Doering, Jan. 2015. "Visibly White: How Community Policing Activists Negotiate Their Whiteness." *Sociology of Race and Ethnicity* 2(1): 106–19.

Dovidio, John F., Brenda Major, and Jennifer Crocker. 2000. "Stigma: Introduction and Overview." In *The Social Psychology of Stigma*, edited by T. F. Heatherton, R. E. Kleck, M. R. Hebl, and J. G. Hull, pp. 1–28. New York: Guilford Press.

DuBois, W. E. B. 1996. "The Souls of White Folk." In *The Oxford W.E.B. DuBois Reader*, edited by Eric J. Sundquist, pp. 497–509. New York: Oxford University Press.

Edin, Kathryn and Laura Lein. 1997. *Making Ends Meet: How Single Mothers Survive Welfare and Low-Wage Work*. New York: Russell Sage Foundation.

Englund, Michelle M., Amy E. Luckner, Gloria J. L. Whaley, and Byron Egeland. 2004. "Children's Achievement in Early Elementary School: Longitudinal Effects of Parental Involvement, Expectations, and Quality of Assistance." *Journal of Educational Psychology* 96(4): 723–30.

Ezekiel, Raphael S. 2002. "An Ethnographer Looks at Neo-Nazi and Klan Groups: The Racist Mind Revisited." *American Behavioral Scientist* 46(1): 51–71.

Feagin, Joe R. 2013. *The White Racial Frame: Centuries of Racial Framing and Counter-Framing*. London: Routledge.

Feagin, Joe R. and Eileen O'Brien. 2003. *White Men on Race*. Boston, MA: Beacon Press.

Federal Bureau of Investigation. 2018. "2017 Hate Crime Statistics." https://ucr.fbi.gov/hate-crime/2017.

Fiske, Susan T. 2011. *Envy Up, Scorn Down: How Status Divides Us*. New York: Russell Sage Foundation.

Flagg, Barbara J. 2005. "Whiteness as Metaprivilege: Some Critical Perspectives: Foreword." *Washington University Journal of Law & Policy* 18: 1–12.

Flores, Nelson. 2016. "A Tale of Two Visions: Hegemonic Whiteness and Bilingual Education." *Educational Policy* 30(1): 13–38.

Flores, Lisa A. and Dreama G. Moon. 2002. "Rethinking Race, Revealing Dilemmas: Imagining a New Racial Subject in Race Traitor." *Western Journal of Communication* 66(2): 181–207.

Ford, Kristie A. and Josephine Orlandella. 2015. "The 'Not-So-Final Remark': The Journey to Becoming White Allies." *Sociology of Race and Ethnicity* 1(2): 287–301.

Foremost Insurance Group. n.d. "2012 Mobile Home Market Facts." http://docplayer.net/9019366-2012-mobile-home-market-facts.html.

Formisano, Ronald P. 1991. *Boston against Busing: Race, Class, and Ethnicity in the 1960s and 1970s*. Chapel Hill: University of North Carolina Press.

Fox, Cybelle and Thomas A. Guglielmo. 2012. "Defining America's Racial Boundaries: Blacks, Mexicans, and European Immigrants, 1890–1945." *American Journal of Sociology* 118(2): 327–79.

Frankenburg, Ruth. 1993. *White Women, Race Matters: The Social Construction of Whiteness*. Minneapolis: University of Minnesota Press.

Franks, Peter, Peter Muennig, Erica Lubetkin, and Haomiao Jia. 2006. "The Burden of Disease Associated with Being African-American in the United States and the Contribution of Socio-Economic Status." *Social Science & Medicine* 62(10): 2469–78.

Frey, William H. 2019. "Less Than Half of US Children under 15 Are White, Census Shows." Brookings. https://www.brookings.edu/research/less-than-half-of-us-children-under-15-are-white-census-shows.

Gallagher, Charles Andrew and France Winddance Twine, eds. 2012. *Retheorizing Race and Whiteness in the 21st Century: Changes and Challenges*. London: Routledge.

Galonnier, Juliette. 2015. "The Racialization of Muslims in France and the United States: Some Insights from White Converts to Islam." *Social Compass* 62(4): 570–83.

Gans, Herbert J. 2012. "Whitening and the Changing American Racial Hierarchy." *DuBois Review* 9: 267–79.

Gest, Justin. 2016. *The New Minority: White Working Class Politics in an Age of Immigration and Inequality*. New York: Oxford University Press.

Gilens, Martin. 1996. "Race and Poverty In America: Public Misperceptions and the American News Media." *Public Opinion Quarterly* 60(4): 515–41.

Goffman, Erving. 1963. *Stigma: Notes on the Management of a Spoiled Identity.* New York: Simon & Schuster.

Golbeck, Natasha and Wendy D. Roth. 2012. "Aboriginal Claims: DNA Ancestry Testing and Changing Concepts of Indigeneity." In *Biomapping Indigenous Peoples: Towards an Understanding of the Issues,* edited by S. Berthier-Foglar, S. Collingwood-Whittick, and S. Tolazzi, pp. 415–32. Amsterdam: Rodopi.

Goren, Matt J. and Victoria C. Plaut. 2012. "Identity Form Matters: White Racial Identity and Attitudes toward Diversity." *Self and Identity* 11(2): 237–54.

Gramsci, Antonio. 1971. *Selections from the Prison Notebooks of Antonio Gramsci.* New York: International Publishers.

Green, Donald P., Dara Z. Strolovitch, and Janelle S. Wong. 1998. "Defended Neighborhoods, Integration, and Racially Motivated Crime." *American Journal of Sociology* 104(2): 372–403.

Griffin, John Howard. 1961. *Black Like Me.* Boston, MA: Houghton Mifflin.

Grollman, Eric Anthony. 2018. "Sexual Orientation Differences in Whites' Racial Attitudes." *Sociological Forum* 33(1): 186–210.

Guglielmo, Thomas A. 2003. *White on Arrival: Italians, Race, Color, and Power in Chicago, 1890–1945.* New York: Oxford University Press.

Hagerman, Margaret Ann. 2014. "White Families and Race: Colour-Blind and Colour-Conscious Approaches to White Racial Socialization." *Ethnic and Racial Studies* 37(14): 2598–614.

Hagerman, Margaret Ann. 2017. "White Racial Socialization: Progressive Fathers on Raising 'Antiracist' Children." *Journal of Marriage and Family* 79(1): 60–74.

Hagerman, Margaret A. 2018. *White Kids: Growing Up with Privilege in a Racially Divided America.* New York: NYU Press.

Hague, Euan and Edward H. Sebesta. 2009. "Neo-Confederacy and the Understanding of Race." In *Neo-Confederacy: A Critical Introduction,* edited by Euan Hague, Edward H.

Sebesta and Heidi Beirich, pp. 131–66. Austin: University of Texas Press.

Hardie, Jessica Halliday and Karolyn Tyson. 2013. "Other People's Racism: Race, Rednecks, and Riots in a Southern High School." *Sociology of Education* 86(1): 83–102.

Hartigan, John. 2003. "Who Are These White People? 'Rednecks,' 'Hillbillies,' and 'White Trash' as Marked Racial Subjects." In *White Out: The Continuing Significance of Racism*, edited by Ashley W. Doane and Eduardo Bonilla-Silva, pp. 95–112. New York: Routledge.

Hartigan, John, Jr. 1997. "Establishing the Fact of Whiteness." *American Anthropologist* 99(3): 495–505.

Hartigan, John, Jr. 1999. *Racial Situations: Class Predicaments of Whiteness in Detroit*. Princeton, NJ: Princeton University Press.

Hartigan, John, Jr. 2004. "Whiteness and Appalachian Studies: What's the Connection?" *Journal of Appalachian Studies* 10(1/2): 58–72.

Hartmann, Douglas, Paul R. Croll, Ryan Larson, Joseph Gerteis, and Alex Manning. 2017. "Colorblindness as Identity: Key Determinants, Relations to Ideology, and Implications for Attitudes about Race and Policy." *Sociological Perspectives* 60(5): 866–88.

Hartmann, Douglas, Joseph Gerteis, and Paul R. Croll. 2009. "An Empirical Assessment of Whiteness Theory: Hidden from How Many?" *Social Problems* 56(3): 403–24.

Hawley, George. 2017. *Making Sense of the Alt-Right*. New York: Columbia University Press.

Helms, Janet E. 1990. *Black and White Racial Identity: Theory, Research, and Practice*. New York: Greenwood Press.

Henderson, Geraldine Rosa, Jerome D. Williams, Anne-Marie Hakstian, and Brian D. Behnken. 2016. *Consumer Equality: Race and the American Marketplace*. Santa Barbara, CA: ABC-CLIO.

Herman, Melissa. 2004. "Forced to Choose: Some Determinants of Racial Identification in Multiracial Adolescents." *Child Development* 75(3): 730–48.

Hochschild, Jennifer. 2006. "When Do People Not Protest Unfairness? The Case of Skin Color Discrimination." *Social Research* 73(2): 473–98.

Howell, Susan E. and Deborah Fagan. 1988. "Race and Trust

In Government: Testing the Political Reality Model." *Public Opinion Quarterly* 52(3): 343–50.

Hughey, Matthew W. 2010. "The (Dis)Similarities of White Racial Identities: The Conceptual Framework of 'Hegemonic Whiteness.'" *Ethnic and Racial Studies* 33(8): 1289–309.

Hughey, Matthew W. 2012a. "Stigma Allure and White Antiracist Identity Management." *Social Psychology Quarterly* 75(3): 219–41.

Hughey, Matthew W. 2012b. *White Bound: Nationalists, Antiracists, and the Shared Meanings of Race.* Palo Alto, CA: Stanford University Press.

Hughey, Matthew W. and W. Carson Byrd. 2013. "The Souls of White Folk beyond Formation and Structure: Bound to Identity." *Ethnic and Racial Studies* 36(6): 974–81.

Hughes, Michael, K. Jill Kiecolt, Verna M. Keith, and David H. Demo. 2015. "Racial Identity and Well-Being among African Americans." *Social Psychology Quarterly* 78(1): 25–48.

Ignatiev, Noel. 1995. *How the Irish Became White.* New York: Routledge.

Ignatiev, Noel, and John Garvey. 2007. "Abolish the White Race by Any Means Necessary," in J. F. Healey and E. O'Brien, eds., *Race, Ethnicity, and Gender: Selected Readings*, pp. 448–51. Los Angeles, CA: Pine Forge Press.

Jacobson, Matthew Frye. 1999. *Whiteness of a Different Color: European Immigrants and the Alchemy of Race.* Cambridge, MA: Harvard University Press.

Jacobson, Matthew Frye. 2006. *Roots Too: White Ethnic Revival in Post-Civil Rights America.* Cambridge, MA: Harvard University Press.

Jardina, Ashley. 2019. *White Identity Politics.* Cambridge: Cambridge University Press.

Jenkins, Morris, Eric G. Lambert, and David N. Baker. 2009. "The Attitudes of Black and White College Students toward Gays and Lesbians." *Journal of Black Studies* 39(4): 589–613.

Jiménez, Tomás R. 2010. "Affiliative Ethnic Identity: A More Elastic Link between Ethnic Ancestry and Culture." *Ethnic and Racial Studies* 33(10): 1756–75.

Jiménez, Tomás R., Corey D. Fields, and Ariela Schachter. 2015. "How Ethnoraciality Matters: Looking Inside Ethnoracial 'Groups.'" *Social Currents* 2(2): 107–15.

Jiménez, Tomás R. and Adam L. Horowitz. 2013. "When

White Is Just Alright: How Immigrants Redefine Achievement and Reconfigure the Ethnoracial Hierarchy." *American Sociological Review* 33: 1756–75.

Karabel, Jerome. 2005. *The Chosen: The Hidden History of Admission and Exclusion at Harvard, Yale, and Princeton.* Boston, MA: Houghton Mifflin.

Kefalas, Maria. 2003. *Working-Class Heroes: Protecting Home, Community, and Nation in a Chicago Neighborhood.* Berkeley: University of California Press.

Kennedy, N. Brent. 1994. *The Melungeons: The Resurrection of a Proud People: An Untold Story of Ethnic Cleansing in America.* Macon, GA: Mercer University Press.

Kimmel, Michael S. and Abby L. Ferber, eds. 2009. *Privilege: A Reader.* Boulder, CO: Westview Press.

Kinder, Donald R. and Lynn M. Sanders. 1996. *Divided by Color: Racial Politics and Democratic Ideals.* Chicago, IL: University of Chicago Press.

Kleinman, Arthur and Rachel Hall-Clifford. 2009. "Stigma: A Social, Cultural and Moral Process." *Journal of Epidemiology and Community Health* 63(6): 418–19.

Kluegel, James R. and Eliot R. Smith. 1983. "Affirmative Action Attitudes: Effects of Self-Interest, Racial Affect, and Stratification Beliefs on Whites' Views." *Social Forces* 61(3): 797–824.

Knowles, Eric D., Brian S. Lowery, Rosalind M. Chow, and Miguel M. Unzueta. 2014. "Deny, Distance, or Dismantle? How White Americans Manage a Privileged Identity." *Perspectives on Psychological Science* 9(6): 594–609.

Knowles, Eric D., Brian S. Lowery, Caitlin M. Hogan, and Rosalind M. Chow. 2009. "On the Malleability of Ideology: Motivated Construals of Color Blindness." *Journal of Personality and Social Psychology* 96(4): 857–69.

Korver-Glenn, Elizabeth. 2018. "Compounding Inequalities: How Racial Stereotypes and Discrimination Accumulate across the Stages of Housing Exchange." *American Sociological Review* 83(4): 627–56.

Kosic, Ankica and Karen Phalet. 2006. "Ethnic Categorization of Immigrants: The Role of Prejudice, Perceived Acculturation Strategies and Group Size." *International Journal of Intercultural Relations* 30(6): 769–82.

Kramer, Rory, Ruth Burke, and Camille Z. Charles. 2015. "When

Change Doesn't Matter: Racial Identity (In)Consistency and Adolescent Well-Being." *Sociology of Race and Ethnicity* 1(2): 270–86.

Krivo, Lauren and Robert Kaufman. 2004. "Housing and Wealth Inequality: Racial–Ethnic Differences in Home Equity in the United States." *Demography* 41(3): 585–605.

Krysan, Maria. 2000. "Prejudice, Politics, and Public Opinion: Understanding the Sources of Racial Policy Attitudes." *Annual Review of Sociology* 26(1): 135–68.

Kusenbach, Margarethe. 2009. "Salvaging Decency: Mobile Home Residents' Strategies of Managing the Stigma of 'Trailer' Living." *Qualitative Sociology* 32(4): 399–428.

Ladd, Helen F. 1998. "Evidence on Discrimination in Mortgage Lending." *Journal of Economic Perspectives* 12(2): 41–62.

Lareau, Annette. 2003. *Unequal Childhoods*. Berkeley: University of California Press.

League of American Orchestras. 2016. *Racial/Ethnic and Gender Diversity in the Orchestra Field*. http://www.ppv.issuelab.org/resources/25840/25840.pdf.

Levine-Rasky, Cynthia. 2016. *Whiteness Fractured*. New York: Routledge.

Lewis, Amanda E. 2003. *Race in the Schoolyard: Negotiating the Color Line in Classrooms and Communities*. New Brunswick, NJ: Rutgers University Press.

Lewis, Amanda E. 2004. "'What Group?' Studying Whites and Whiteness in the Era of 'Color-Blindness.'" *Sociological Theory* 22(4): 623–46.

Liebler, Carolyn A., Sonya R. Porter, Leticia E. Fernandez, James M. Noon, and Sharon R. Ennis. 2017. "America's Churning Races: Race and Ethnicity Response Changes Between Census 2000 and the 2010 Census." *Demography* 54(1): 259–84.

Liebler, Carolyn A. and Meghan Zacher. 2013. "American Indians without Tribes in the Twenty-First Century." *Ethnic and Racial Studies* 36(11): 1910–34.

Link, Bruce G. and Jo C. Phelan. 2001. "Conceptualizing Stigma." *Annual Review of Sociology* 27(1): 363–85.

López, Ian Haney. 2006 [1996]. *White by Law 10th Anniversary Edition: The Legal Construction of Race* (rev. 10th anniversary edn.). New York: NYU Press.

Low, Setha. 2009. "Maintaining Whiteness: The Fear of Others and Niceness." *Transforming Anthropology* 17(2): 79–92.

McCarty, William P. 2010. "Trailers and Trouble? An Examination of Crime in Mobile Home Communities." *Cityscape* 12(2): 127–44.

McDermott, Monica. 2006. *Working-Class White: The Making and Unmaking of Race Relations*. Berkeley: University of California Press.

McDermott, Monica. 2010. "Ways of Being White: Privilege, Perceived Stigma, and Transcendence." In *Doing Race: 21 Essays for the 21st Century*, edited by H. R. Markus and P. Moya, pp. 415–38. New York: W. W. Norton.

McDermott, Monica. 2015. "Color-Blind and Color-Visible Identity among American Whites." *American Behavioral Scientist* 59(11): 1452–73.

McDermott, Monica, Eric D. Knowles, and Jennifer A. Richeson. 2019. "Class Perceptions and Attitudes toward Immigration and Race among Working-Class Whites." *Analyses of Social Issues and Public Policy* 19(1): 349–80.

Macias, Thomas. 2016. "Environmental Risk Perception among Race and Ethnic Groups in the United States." *Ethnicities* 16(1): 111–29.

McKinney, Karyn D. and Joe R. Feagin. 2004. *Being White: Stories of Race and Racism*. London: Routledge.

MacLean, Nancy. 1995. *Behind the Mask of Chivalry: The Making of the Second Ku Klux Klan*. New York: Oxford University Press.

MacTavish, Katherine A. 2006. "We're Like the Wrong Side of the Tracks: Upscale Suburban Development, Social Inequality, and Rural Mobile Home Park Residence". RPRC Working Paper No. 06–03. Columbia, MO: Rural Poverty Research Center.

McVeigh, Rory. 2009. *The Rise of the Ku Klux Klan: Right-Wing Movements and National Politics*. Minneapolis: University of Minnesota Press.

Major, Brenda and Laurie T. O'Brien. 2005. "The Social Psychology of Stigma." *Annual Review of Psychology* 56(1): 393–421.

Maly, Michael and Heather Dalmage. 2015. *Vanishing Eden: White Construction of Memory, Meaning, and Identity in a Racially Changing City*. Philadelphia, PA: Temple University Press.

Mann, Geoff. 2008. "Why Does Country Music Sound White?

Race and the Voice of Nostalgia." *Ethnic and Racial Studies* 31(1): 73–100.

Mann, Geoff. 2012. "Why Does Country Music Sound White? Race and the Voice of Nostalgia." In *Retheorizing Race and Whiteness in the 21st Century: Changes and Challenges*, edited by C. Gallagher and F. W. Twine, pp. 69–96. London: Routledge.

Markowitz, Fred E. 2005. "Sociological Models of Mental Illness Stigma: Progress and Prospects." In *On the Stigma of Mental Illness: Practical Strategies for Research and Social Change*, edited by P. W. Corrigan, pp. 129–44. Washington, DC: American Psychological Association.

Marshburn, Christopher K. and Eric D. Knowles. 2018. "White Out of Mind: Identity Suppression as a Coping Strategy among Whites Anticipating Racially Charged Interactions." *Group Processes & Intergroup Relations* 21(6): 874–92.

Martin, Judith N., Robert L. Krizek, Thomas L. Nakayama, and Lisa Bradford. 1999. "What Do White People Want to Be Called? A Study of Self-Labels for White Americans." In *Whiteness: The Communication of a Social Identity*, edited by T. L. Nakayama and J. N. Martin, pp. 27–50. Thousand Oaks, CA: SAGE.

Massey, Douglas S., Jacob S. Rugh, Justin P. Steil, and Len Albright. 2016. "Riding the Stagecoach to Hell: A Qualitative Analysis of Racial Discrimination in Mortgage Lending." *City & Community* 15(2): 118–36.

Mather, Darin M., Stephen W. Jones, and Scott Moats. 2017. "Improving upon Bogardus: Creating a More Sensitive and Dynamic Social Distance Scale." *Survey Practice* 10(4). doi: 10.29115/SP-2017-0026.

Maxwell, Angie and T. Wayne Parent. 2012. "The Obama Trigger: Presidential Approval and Tea Party Membership." *Social Science Quarterly* 93(5): 1384–401.

Mercer, Sterett H. and Michael Cunningham. 2003. "Racial Identity in White American College Students: Issues of Conceptualization and Measurement." *Journal of College Student Development* 44(2): 217–30.

Metzl, Jonathan M. 2019. *Dying of Whiteness: How the Politics of Racial Resentment Is Killing America's Heartland*. New York: Basic Books.

Miller, Carol T. and Cheryl R. Kaiser. 2001. "A Theoretical

Perspective on Coping with Stigma." *Journal of Social Issues* 57(1): 73–92.

Miller, Paula K. 2016. "'But Aren't We All Poor?' How Whites' Perceptions of Economic Group Threat Influence Racial Attitudes in Michigan." *Michigan Sociological Review* 30: 44–68.

Morning, Ann. 2018. "Kaleidoscope: Contested Identities and New Forms of Race Membership." *Ethnic and Racial Studies* 41(6): 1055–73.

Morris, Edward W. 2012. "Repelling the 'Rutter': Social Differentiation Among Rural Teenagers." *Symbolic Interaction* 35(3): 301–20.

Moss, Kirby. 2003. *The Color of Class: Poor Whites and the Paradox of Privilege*. Philadelphia: University of Pennsylvania Press.

Nagel, Joane. 1995. "American Indian Ethnic Renewal: Politics and the Resurgence of Identity." *American Sociological Review* 60(6): 947–65.

Nakayama, Thomas K. and Judith N. Martin, eds. 1999. *Whiteness: The Communication of Social Identity*. Thousand Oaks, CA: SAGE.

Newitz, Annalee and Matthew Wray. 1997. "What Is 'White Trash'? Sterotypes and Economic Conditions of Poor Whites in the United States." In *Whiteness: A Critical Reader*, edited by M. Hill, pp. 151–67. New York: NYU Press.

Oliver, J. Eric and Tali Mendelberg. 2000. "Reconsidering the Environmental Determinants of White Racial Attitudes." *American Journal of Political Science* 44(3): 574–89.

Omi, Michael A. 2001. "The Changing Meaning of Race." In *America Becoming: Racial Trends and their Consequences*, edited by N. J. Smelser, W. J. Wilson, and F. Mitchell, vol. 1, pp. 243–63. Washington, DC: National Research Council.

Pahlke, Erin, Rebecca S. Bigler, and Marie-Anne Suizzo. 2012. "Relations between Colorblind Socialization and Children's Racial Bias: Evidence From European American Mothers and Their Preschool Children." *Child Development* 83(4): 1164–79.

Painter, Nell Irvin. 2011. *The History of White People*. New York: W. W. Norton.

Peffley, Mark and Jon Hurwitz. 2002. "The Racial Components of 'Race-Neutral' Crime Policy Attitudes." *Political Psychology* 23(1): 59–75.

Perry, Andre, Jonathan Rothwell, and David Harshbarger. 2018. "The Devaluation of Assets in Black Neighborhoods: The Case of Residential Property." Brookings. https://www.brookings.edu/research/devaluation-of-assets-in-black-neighborhoods.

Perry, Pamela. 2001. "White Means Never Having to Say You're Ethnic: White Youth and the Construction of 'Cultureless' Identities." *Journal of Contemporary Ethnography* 30(1): 56–91.

Perry, Pamela. 2002. *Shades of White: White Kids and Racial Identities in High School*. Durham, NC: Duke University Press.

Phinney, Jean S. 1989. "Stages of Ethnic Identity Development in Minority Group Adolescents." *Journal of Early Adolescence* 9(1/2): 34–49.

Pickett, Justin T. and Ted Chiricos. 2012. "Controlling Other People's Children: Racialized Views of Delinquency and Whites' Punitive Attitudes toward Juvenile Offenders." *Criminology* 50(3): 673–710.

Powell-Hopson, Darlene and Derek S. Hopson. 1988. "Implications of Doll Color Preferences among Black Preschool Children and White Preschool Children." *Journal of Black Psychology* 14(2): 57–63.

Richeson, Jennifer A. and J. Nicole Shelton. 2007. "Negotiating Interracial Interactions: Costs, Consequences, and Possibilities." *Current Directions in Psychological Science* 16(6): 316–20.

Rieder, Jonathan. 1985. *Canarsie*. Cambridge, MA: Harvard University Press.

Rocha, Rene R. and Rodolfo Espino. 2009. "Racial Threat, Residential Segregation, and the Policy Attitudes of Anglos." *Political Research Quarterly* 62(2): 415–26.

Rockquemore, Kerry and David L. Brunsma. 2002. *Beyond Black: Biracial Identity in America*. Thousand Oaks, CA; London: SAGE.

Rodriquez, Jason. 2006. "Color-Blind Ideology and the Cultural Appropriation of Hip-Hop." *Journal of Contemporary Ethnography* 35(6): 645–68.

Roediger, David. 1991. *The Wages of Whiteness: Race and the Making of the American Working Class*. London: Verso.

Romero, Mary. 2018. *Introducing Intersectionality*. Cambridge: Polity.

Rosenthal, Lisa, Ashleigh Deosaran, DaSean L. Young, and Tyrel J. Starks. 2019. "Relationship Stigma and Well-Being among Adults in Interracial and Same-Sex Relationships." *Journal of Social and Personal Relationships* 36(11/12): 3408–28.

Roth, Wendy D. and Biorn Ivemark. 2018. "Genetic Options: The Impact of Genetic Ancestry Testing on Consumers' Racial and Ethnic Identities." *American Journal of Sociology* 124(1): 150–84.

Rothenberg, Paula S., ed. 2002. *White Privilege: Essential Readings on the Other Side of Racism.* New York: Worth Publishers.

Rothstein, Richard. 2017. *The Color of Law: A Forgotten History of How Our Government Segregated America.* New York: Liveright Publishing Corporation.

Royster, Deirdre. 2003. *Race and the Invisible Hand: How White Networks Exclude Black Men from Blue-Collar Jobs.* Berkeley: University of California Press.

Samson, Frank L. 2013. "Multiple Group Threat and Malleable White Attitudes towards Academic Merit." *Du Bois Review: Social Science Research on Race* 10(1): 233–60.

Samson, Frank L. and Lawrence D. Bobo. 2014. "Ethno-Racial Attitudes and Social Inequality." In *Handbook of the Social Psychology of Inequality*, edited by J. D. McLeod, E. J. Lawler, and M. Schwalbe, pp. 515–45. Dordrecht: Springer Netherlands.

Sanua, Marianne R. 2018. *Going Greek: Jewish College Fraternities in the United States, 1895–1945.* Detroit, MI: Wayne State University Press.

Schildkraut, Deborah J. 2017. "White Attitudes about Descriptive Representation in the US: The Roles of Identity, Discrimination, and Linked Fate." *Politics, Groups, and Identities* 5(1): 84–106.

Schroer, Todd. 2008. "Technical Advances in Communication: The Example of White Racialist 'Love Groups' and 'White Civil Rights Organizations.'" In *Identity Work in Social Movements*, edited by J. Reger, R. L. Einwohner, and D. J. Myers, pp. 77–99. Minneapolis: University of Minnesota Press.

Shirley, Carla D. 2010. "'You Might Be a Redneck If…' Boundary Work among Rural, Southern Whites." *Social Forces* 89(1): 35–61.

Sinclair, Stacey, Elizabeth Dunn, and Brian Lowery. 2005. "The Relationship between Parental Racial Attitudes and Children's Implicit Prejudice." *Journal of Experimental Social Psychology* 41(3): 283–9.

Skinner, Allison L. and Andrew N. Meltzoff. 2019. "Childhood Experiences and Intergroup Biases among Children." *Social Issues and Policy Review* 13(1): 211–40.

Skocpol, Theda and Vanessa Williamson. 2016. *The Tea Party and the Remaking of Republican Conservatism.* New York: Oxford University Press.

Skrentny, John David. 1996. *The Ironies of Affirmative Action: Politics, Culture, and Justice in America.* Chicago, IL: University of Chicago Press.

Small, Mario Luis, David J. Harding, and Michèle Lamont. 2010. "Introduction: Reconsidering Culture and Poverty." *Annals of the American Academy of Political and Social Science* 629: 6–27.

Solórzano, Daniel G. and Armida Ornelas. 2002. "A Critical Race Analysis of Advanced Placement Classes: A Case of Educational Inequality." *Journal of Latinos and Education* 1(4): 215–29.

Soss, Joe and Vesla Weaver. 2017. "Police Are Our Government: Politics, Political Science, and the Policing of Race/Class Subjugated Communities." *Annual Review of Political Science* 20(1): 565–91.

Spanierman, Lisa B., Patton O. Garriott, and D. Anthony Clark. 2013. "Whiteness and Social Class: Intersections and Implications." In *The Oxford Handbook of Social Class in Counseling*, edited by William Ming Liu, pp. 394–410. New York: Oxford University Press.

Stangor, Charles and Christian S. Crandall. 2000. "Threat and the Social Construction of Stigma." In *The Social Psychology of Stigma*, edited by T. F. Heatherton, pp. 62–87. New York: Guilford Press.

The State. 2019. "SC White Man Who Tried to Hire a KKK Hit Man to Kill Black Neighbor Gets 10 Years." *The State.* https://www.thestate.com/news/local/crime/article229087559.html.

Stoll, Laurie Cooper and Megan Klein. 2018. "'Not in My Backyard': How Abstract Liberalism and Colorblind Diversity Undermines Racial Justice." In *Challenging the Status Quo:*

Diversity, Democracy, and Equality in the 21st Century, edited by S. M. Collins, M. S. Dodson, and D. G. Embrick, pp. 217–40. Leiden: Brill.

Storrs, Debbie. 1999. "Whiteness as Stigma: Essentialist Identity Work by Mixed-Race Women." *Symbolic Interaction* 22(3): 187–212.

Strickler, Jennifer and Nicholas L. Danigelis. 2002. "Changing Frameworks in Attitudes toward Abortion." *Sociological Forum* 17(2): 187–201.

Sullivan, Esther. 2018. *Manufactured Insecurity: Mobile Home Parks and Americans' Tenuous Right to Place*. Oakland: University of California Press.

Sundquist, Eric J., ed. 1996. *The Oxford W. E. B. Du Bois Reader*. New York: Oxford University Press.

Tarman, Christopher and David O. Sears. 2005. "The Conceptualization and Measurement of Symbolic Racism." *The Journal of Politics* 67(3): 731–61.

Tonry, Michael and Matthew Melewski. 2008. "The Malign Effects of Drug and Crime Control Policies on Black Americans." *Crime and Justice* 37(1): 1–44.

Torkelson, Jason and Douglas Hartmann. 2010. "White Ethnicity in Twenty-First-Century America: Findings from a New National Survey." *Ethnic and Racial Studies* 33(8): 1310–31.

Torkelson, Jason and Douglas Hartmann. 2019. "The Racialization of Ethnicity: The New Face of White Ethnicity in Postmillennial America." *Sociology of Race and Ethnicity*. doi:10.1177/2332649219892621.

Tropp, Linda R. and Fiona Kate Barlow. 2018. "Making Advantaged Racial Groups Care about Inequality: Intergroup Contact as a Route to Psychological Investment." *Current Directions in Psychological Science* 27(3): 194–9.

Tuch, Steven A. and Michael Hughes. 2011. "Whites' Racial Policy Attitudes in the Twenty-First Century: The Continuing Significance of Racial Resentment." *Annals of the American Academy of Political and Social Science* 634(1): 134–52.

Twine, France Winddance and Charles Gallagher. 2008. "The Future of Whiteness: A Map of the 'Third Wave.'" *Ethnic and Racial Studies* 31(1): 4–24.

Van Ausdale, Debra and Joe R. Feagin. 2001. *The First R: How*

Children Learn Race and Racism. Lanham, MD: Rowman & Littlefield.

Vasquez, Jessica M. 2014. "Race Cognizance and Colorblindness: Effects of Latino/Non-Hispanic White Intermarriage." *Du Bois Review: Social Science Research on Race* 11(2): 273–93.

Vera, Hernan and Andrew Gordon. 2003. *Screen Saviors: Hollywood Fictions of Whiteness*. Lanham, MD: Rowman & Littlefield.

Vespa, Jonathan, David M. Armstrong, and Lauren Medina. 2018. *Demographic Turning Points for the United States: Population Projections for 2020 to 2060*. Washington, DC: US Census Bureau.

Wade, Wyn Craig. 1998. *The Fiery Cross: The Ku Klux Klan in America*. New York: Oxford University Press.

Ward, Jane. 2008. "White Normativity: The Cultural Dimensions of Whiteness in a Racially Diverse LGBT Organization." *Sociological Perspectives* 51(3): 563–86.

Wark, Colin and John Galliher. 2007. "Emory Bogardus and the Origins of the Social Distance Scale." *American Sociologist* 38(4): 383–95.

Warren, Jonathan W. and France Winddance Twine. 1997. "White Americans, the New Minority? Non-Blacks and the Ever-Expanding Boundaries of Whiteness." *Journal of Black Studies* 28(2): 200–18.

Warren, Patricia, Donald Tomaskovic-Devey, William Smith, Matthew Zingraff, and Marcinda Mason. 2006. "Driving While Black: Bias Processes and Racial Disparity in Police Stops." *Criminology* 44(3): 709–38.

Waters, Mary C. 1990. *Ethnic Options: Choosing Identities in America*. Berkeley: University of California Press.

Webster, Colin. 2008. "Marginalized White Ethnicity, Race and Crime." *Theoretical Criminology* 12(3): 293–312.

White, Karletta M. 2015. "The Salience of Skin Tone: Effects on the Exercise of Police Enforcement Authority." *Ethnic and Racial Studies* 38(6): 993–1010.

Williams, Joan C. 2017. *White Working Class: Overcoming Class Cluelessness in America*. Boston, MA: Harvard Business Press.

Wilson, David C. and Darren W. Davis. 2011. "Reexamining Racial Resentment: Conceptualization and Content." *Annals of the American Academy of Political and Social Science* 634: 117–33.

Wray, Matt. 2019. "A Typology of White People in America." In *The Intersections of Whiteness*, edited by E. Kindinger and M. Schmitt, pp. 38–52. New York: Routledge.

Yang, Mina. 2007. "East Meets West in the Concert Hall: Asians and Classical Music in the Century of Imperialism, Post-Colonialism, and Multiculturalism." *Asian Music* 38(1): 1–30.

Yoxall, Peter. 2006. "The Minuteman Project, Gone in a Minute or Here to Stay: The Origin, History and Future of Citizen Activism on the United States–Mexico Border." *University of Miami Inter-American Law Review* 37: 517–611.

Zernike, Kate. 2010. *Boiling Mad: Inside Tea Party America*. New York: Times Books/Henry Holt and Co.

Zirkel, Sabrina. 2005. "Ongoing Issues of Racial and Ethnic Stigma in Education 50 Years after Brown v. Board." *Urban Review* 37(2): 107–26.

Index